Grammar Lessons and Strategies That Strengthen Students' Writing

Laura Robb

NEW YORK • TORONTO • LONDON • AUCKLAND • SYDNEY
MEXICO CITY • NEW DELHI • HONG KONG

Cover design by Joni Holst
Interior design by Solutions by Design, Inc.

ISBN 0-439- 11758-5

Other Books by Laura Robb

Reading Strategies That Work

Easy-to-Manage Reading and Writing Conferences

Easy Mini-Lessons for Teaching Vocabulary

Brighten Up Boring Beginnings and Other Quick Writing Lessons

Teaching Reading in the Middle School

35 Must-Have Assessment and Record-Keeping Forms for Reading

52 Fabulous Discussion Prompt Cards for Reading Groups

Redefining Staff Development: A Collaborative Model for Teachers and Administrators

Table of Contents

Part III

Editing for Punctuation and Usage

Dedication

With love for Evan and Cookie and Rob and Anina

Acknowledgments

To all the students and teachers with whom I have learned, my deepest thanks for sharing your frustrations over the disconnect between writing and grammar. Your candid dissatisfaction with grammar textbooks and workbooks as well as my own experiences have inspired me to search for alternative methods of teaching grammar and punctuation.

My reading/writing workshop students have provided me with feedback as I developed mini-lessons and pointed to areas of grammar, such as diagramming sentences and memorizing linking verbs, that did not affect their writing. Together, we searched for strategies and ideas that enabled them to recognize their rewrite choices and revise well.

To Wendy Murray, my extraordinary editor, thanks for your patience, understanding, nurturing, and mostly for encouraging me to craft a book that departs from tradition yet has strong research to back up its underlying principles. Always available for questions and support, you have guided the direction of this book with care and enthusiasm. My deepest appreciation also to Joanna Davis-Swing, who carried this manuscript through additional revisions. Your insights and nurturing ways made the process joyful.

To my husband, Lloyd, my thanks for always listening to me talk through an issue and for never grumbling about the long hours I spent writing and researching this book.

Linking Grammar and Punctuation to Writing

When I went to school, an ocean separated my knowledge of grammar and its connection to the writing process. In fourth and fifth grades, I memorized the parts of speech and their definitions, and completed worksheets that asked me to underline a noun, verb, adverb, or adjective. In junior high, I devoted more time to diagramming sentences than to writing. For me and my classmates, grammar was a dull subject that had to be endured.

My first year of teaching, I bristled as I leafed through a sixth-grade grammar and punctuation workbook. Instantly, my memory reclaimed every negative feeling toward those exercises. How surprised I was when students begged to complete the workbooks I had stacked at the bottom of a bookcase. They told me, "It's easy," "We like to underline," and "Once you figure out the pattern, you get a good grade." Ironically, punctuation errors dominated their writing. They used weak verbs such as *get* and *make* and general nouns such as *stuff* and *things*. Paragraphing and commas were not evident in their writing. That year I began exploring ways to connect a knowledge of grammar to students' writing. Thirty-seven years later, it's still a work in progress, a topic I reflect on annually.

During my second year of teaching, though I continued to explore other ways to approach grammar, I was bound by a grammar workbook, which was a required part of the fifth-grade language arts curriculum. Three or four times a week, students spent 40 minutes underlining nouns, subjects, predicates, adjectives, direct and indirect objects, and predicate adjectives and nominatives; they also added commas, capital letters, and end-of-sentence punctuation—all in ready-made sentences.

Although students did not mind filling in the pages, I soon became weary of grading worksheets that didn't connect to students' writing. Most completed the patterned pages well because the sentences were far simpler than the ones they composed. Meanwhile, the grammar issues I observed in students' writing—fragments and run-on sentences, missing commas and sentence punctuation, and lack of paragraphing—remained unaddressed.

I imagine that many teachers across the country experienced my frustration with these grammar and punctuation workbooks, and still do. Recently, though, the research presented in Constance Weaver's *Teaching*

Grammar in Context (1996) strongly supported a key finding that is beginning to change classroom practice: Grammar should be taught in the context of reading and writing. Weaver arrived at this conclusion through research conducted in her own classroom and from the classroom research of other teachers who shared their findings in her grammar support group. In fact, in the afterward to her book, Weaver challenges teachers to "join us in our quest for better ways of teaching those aspects of grammar that seem most important to writers."

Lucy Calkins's *The Art of Teaching Writing* and Donald Graves's *A Fresh Look at Writing* also confirmed my early classroom observations about the effects of worksheets on students' writing. All three researchers agreed that for writing to improve, children have to revise and edit their own work.

And my own reflection helped me articulate three significant reasons for students to learn and understand grammar:

1 **Grammar provides teacher and students with a common language that enables them to talk about writing.** For example, I can invite a student to circle five weak verbs in a piece, return to each weak verb, and brainstorm stronger verbs only if we both understand what a verb is.

2 **A knowledge of parts of speech enables students to write with specific details and strong images.** For students to be able to evaluate and change general nouns, ordinary verbs, and overused adjectives in their own pieces, they need to study published authors' use of each part of speech.

3 **An understanding of phrases, participles, and clauses enables students to write engaging, rhythmic prose.** Students must be able to identify these parts of speech and brainstorm alternative ways to open sentences.

Weaver discovered in her research that adults cling to their past school experiences and therefore challenge changes in grammar instruction. Although parents don't create school curriculum, their views do influence how grammar is taught. I learned how deeply entrenched parents' beliefs can be many years ago, when I led two workshops for parents at Powhatan School that focused on how we were teaching grammar. The first occurred in early October, on parents' night. The second was a month later, after parents visited my class over one week. Because integrating grammar into a writing workshop was a major departure from the way grammar had traditionally been taught at Powhatan, attendance was high with concerned parents.

I told them that instead of giving students isolated grammar exercises and sentences to diagram, teachers and I would present mini-lessons that link the study of grammar and punctuation to students' writing. Mini-lessons and practice sessions would also include analyzing the writing of the best children's authors. During workshop, students would apply their new understandings to their own pieces.

Many parents voiced discomfort with this research-tested practice; they worried that their children would not learn the grammar. "I wish you'd teach my child how to diagram sentences from Joseph Conrad's *Lord Jim* instead of doing all this writing-workshop stuff," an agitated parent exclaimed. "I'm sick of seeing messy papers, inserts, arrows. I want a perfect paper first time round, and the way to do that is to learn grammar and diagram sentences from hard books."

How to integrate grammar into writing instruction continues to polarize educators. Those who believe grammar must be taught as a separate subject base their ideas on their own school experiences. I culled the list that follows after asking teachers in a professional development workshop I was giving to brainstorm what the word *grammar* means to them. It hits upon common beliefs of why studying grammar as a separate subject is beneficial:

- Improves writing and sentence structure.

- Develops the ability to reason and think logically, especially through diagramming sentences.

- Teaches punctuation.

- Enables students to be more effective readers and speakers.

- Supports students' study of another language.

In *English Grammar and Composition,* the grammar and composition textbook widely used in middle and high schools, John Warriner states in the introduction: "By studying grammar, you learn how the language works. This knowledge will help you to improve both your writing and your speech… follow the rules, do the practice exercises, and whenever you write or speak put to use what you have learned. You will find your work will improve steadily."

But in my experience as a teacher, the transfer from completing grammar exercises to speech and writing occurs only when teachers help students understand how to apply this knowledge to their writing. In fact, students tend to view grammar and writing as separate subjects. Research studies corroborate student and teachers' experiences (Greene 1950; DeBoer 1959; Searles and Carlson 1960; Calkins 1980, 1983, 1994), demonstrating that there is little correlation between completing grammar and punctuation exercises and progress with writing, speaking, and learning a foreign language.

Contrary to Warriner's charge that students can improve their grammar if they use the rules they've learned when they speak and write, I have observed many students who complete grammar exercises perfectly but are unable to connect this isolated practice to their writing.

Beyond the Grammar Workbook

Although I am still required to teach some traditional grammar at my school, over the years I have found ways to connect the study of grammar to students' reading and writing. I tell my students that my primary goal is to help them become better writers, and that what I teach them about grammar serves this goal. In other words, in all the grammar work we do, I demonstrate how a knowledge of grammatical structures can improve their writing. It can clarify meaning, make revising simpler, and make their prose more fluid and engaging.

With this book, I share with you how I build students' knowledge of grammar principles and punctuation in the context of reading and writing. The list that follows provides an overview of the teaching strategies I describe in greater detail in the pages to come. Each strategy focuses on exploring, understanding, and then linking grammatical knowledge to students' written work.

Mini-Lessons and Strategy Lessons

Use these lessons to make the structure of language and the thinking behind punctuation and repairing sentences accessible to students. By thinking aloud (Lytle 1982; Baumann, Jones, and Seifert-Kessell 1993) as you analyze passages from literature and by modeling how you go about composing and revising, students can hear and see how you notice and use grammar "for real."

Literature

Spotlight grammar and punctuation at work in powerful fiction, nonfiction, and poetry. In addition to the passages you show students, invite them to search books for examples of the concepts you're studying. Often, to introduce a mini-lesson, I share a powerful literary example. After the mini-lesson, while students are practicing a writing strategy, I invite them to bring in literary examples from their independent reading to share the next day. Analyzing outstanding literary examples offers students many opportunities to gain insight into how grammatical structures affect the finest written language.

Word Walls

On a large chart or construction paper, invite students to print examples of parts of speech you're studying, such as strong verbs or specific nouns. These word walls also can include student-composed sentences that illustrate repairing run-ons and fragments or using phrases to vary sentence openings.

Personal Word Collections

In small writers' notebooks, have students collect striking words and phrases from reading books, poems, magazines, and the newspaper.

Forge Grammar-Writing Connections

Invite students to apply grammar principles to their own writing by having them revise for a specific purpose. For example, they may revise to improve verbs, vary sentence openings with clauses, or repair run-ons or fragments.

Mini-Conferences

During writing workshop, circulate around the room and pause at students' desks for a short conference. Use these brief encounters to support students as they attempt to revise and connect what they've learned to their own pieces.

Scaffolding

For students who need extra support linking a concept to their writing, scaffold their learning by working one on one. Sitting side by side, think aloud, modeling for the student how you revise for, say, strong verbs. While you are there to probe with questions and suggestions, ask the student to brainstorm alternative verbs and choose the best one. Continue scaffolding until you think a student can work with a partner and/or independently.

The grammar concepts I focus on in this book, combined with these seven teaching points, enable students to develop their composing, revising, and editing abilities through short writing exercises and their own pieces. But I want to emphasize that in addition to teacher-presented mini-lessons, students benefit from having many mentors so they can learn from teachers, peers, older students, and authors of books they read.

How to Use This Book

I open the school year focusing on the parts of speech, for strong verbs and specific nouns define good writing. However, do not view the book's topics as a sequential time line. Whenever I observe a need among students, I shift gears and address what is proving difficult for them. For example, if many students are writing run-on sentences, then I'll temporarily put aside our study of verbs and present mini-lessons that offer strategies for repairing run-ons. Those students who don't require additional practice work independently on their writing.

The general idea here is to teach grammar with flexibility and to see your students' errors in usage and punctuation as signs of growth and cues to teach rather than as distressing mistakes. With my students, these mistakes tell me that they are experimenting with more complex language and are ready to receive instruction that can move them forward. Adapt the book's contents to your needs and especially to the needs of your students.

Part I includes suggestions for introducing the key parts of speech. Part II focuses on how clauses, participles, and prepositional phrases can improve sentence structure. It also addresses how coordinating conjunctions are useful when combining short sentences with repeated information. Part III reviews paragraphing and basic sentence punctuation and includes a list of standard editing symbols.

Collaborative Strategy Lessons: Demonstrating to Improve Writing

A strategy I often use at the start of and during writing workshop, and one that deepens students' understanding of each concept, is the collaborative strategy lesson. Rather like an extended strategy-lesson, the strategy lesson includes collaborative practice, so that students can have peer support as they try a new grammar "move" while the teacher is available for questions and support.

To illustrate: In a ten- to fifteen-minute strategy lesson that combines the direct teaching and modeling described by Lucy Calkins (1986, 1994) and Nancie Atwell (1987, 1999), students can observe how you use your knowledge of grammar to draft and revise and examine how an author crafted an effective passage. Whether you use an overhead projector and transparencies or large chart paper, make sure there's enough time for students to raise questions and exchange ideas. They'll collect many strategies from one another and apply these to their own pieces.

THREE KINDS OF COLLABORATIVE STRATEGY LESSONS

I have found that it's impossible to continually predict my students' needs and preplan each strategy lesson. By carefully observing them during workshop and as they respond to strategy lessons, I collect strategy lesson topics that I can present to individuals, pairs, or small groups that day so that I quickly respond to students' needs.

1. **Planned Strategy Lessons:** You'll prepare and think through the grammar, editing, or punctuation principle before presenting it.

2. **Impromptu Strategy Lessons:** As you circulate among students and read their pieces, you'll observe a need such as varying sentence openings or repairing fragments. The moment is ripe for an unrehearsed strategy lesson presented to a small or large group.

3. **Review Strategy Lessons:** Throughout the year, as you read students' writing, you'll identify topics that require review. First revisit the strategy lesson and any interactive wall charts you developed, then coach pairs or groups that require support.

Mini-Conferences

Short and focused, lasting one to three minutes, mini-conferences are the ideal way to visit with many students engaged in writing. For more about them, see my book *Easy-to-Manage Reading & Writing Conferences* or Donald Graves's micro-lessons in *A Fresh Look at Writing*. These brief encounters allow you to support a grammar or punctuation issue that the student raises or one you observe. The key to success and brevity is to inform students that you will address only one issue. You'll find that students welcome this tight focus. As one sixth grader put it: "When a teacher tries to help me with commas, paragraphing, changing verbs, and run-ons at the same time, I tune him out."

During a 45-minute period, you will be able to visit with seven to fifteen students. You may repeat a mini-lesson or use the time to scaffold a skill, such as paragraphing or using commas. Begin the conference by raising a question about what you notice a student doing—or not doing—in regard to capitalization, run-on sentences, fragments, varying sentence openings, and so forth. Begin with a question about the issue that seems most crucial. The sample conferences described below show how I choose a conference focus. (They also underscore that often a student may need several ten- to fifteen-minute follow-up conferences to understand a concept.)

Mini-conference with José, a seventh grader

TOPIC: Marking paragraphs

Robb: This memoir is terrific. The story about using a tennis racket instead of a net to catch a bass made me laugh. I noticed, though, that you haven't marked any paragraphs. Can you tell me why?

José: Gosh, I never noticed until now. I guess I was so into the story that I didn't think about that.

Robb: That happens to professional writers, too. Reread your memoir and decide where you think each paragraph starts, using the symbol for paragraph. Then show me your work. Would you like to mark the first two paragraphs with me watching?

José: Okay. [He's successful, and I move on to another student.]

My Observation

Although José also needed coaching on using commas, I chose to focus first on paragraphing because we had been working on this skill and using the editing symbol for "new paragraph" to mark first drafts (see page 86). Often, young writers like José are so intent on the plot of their story that they don't notice that they have a two-page paragraph.

By inviting José to practice in my presence, I learned that he could paragraph. All he needed was a reminder to attend to it and a nudge to begin with me at his side. The purpose of these meetings is to discover what the student can improve, get the student started, and then move on.

If José could not paragraph, I would have sat close by and modeled how I make paragraphing decisions by reading his text aloud and thinking my process aloud. Such scaffolding would continue for three to four more mini-conferences. Then I'd invite José to think aloud and show me his paragraphing strategies. If he was successful, I'd pair José with a peer next time I asked the students to edit for paragraphing. Gradually, I'd move José to independence.

Some students need more than three or four scaffolding meetings. Work with them until they can take over the process. You might have to drop paragraphing for a while as you move on to another topic. However, take every editing opportunity that relates to paragraphing and support students who aren't there yet.

WHAT QUESTION DO I POSE?

The more I read students' work and jot down areas that need support, confer with them, and observe them during mini-lessons and independent writing, the better equipped I am to pose a question that guides a student to select an area he or she can improve. Here are some questions and prompts that work for me. Adapt them to your students.

Questions and Prompts for Guiding Students

◎ Can you find the fragment in your first paragraph?

◎ Look at paragraph two. How many lines is the first sentence? Read it out loud and see if you can hear how you might break it into two sentences.

◎ Have you correctly punctuated the dialogue on the second page? Let's punctuate it together.

◎ There are several paragraphs in this piece. Read it out loud and every time the topic, time, action, or place shifts, consider starting a new paragraph.

◎ Read your first paragraph out loud and circle the word that starts each sentence. Can you use some of the strategies we've practiced to vary the sentence openings?

◎ Have you located the nouns that need apostrophes? How can I help you?

For additional questions and prompts, see pages 79 and 84.

Grade 8

Student's Name	Strengths	Needs
Peter B.	• paragraphs • short snappy title • strong verbs	• organization of ideas • commas
Carl D.	• specific details • shows • lead - a grabber	• work on ending • add dialogue
Penny D.	• strong idea • good plot line • paragraphs	• work on lead • commas
Maria D.	• rich details • strong verbs • tries different kinds of type	• paragraphing • organizing ideas
David K.	• good lead • title - a grabber • shows • paragraphs	• commas • stronger verbs
Susan L.	• poem has shape • strong verbs • good images embedded in lines	• tighten some lines • more specific nouns • figurative lang.
Tommy M.	• poem - good rhyming in each quatrain • similes effective	• stronger verbs • work on tightening lines
Roger M.	• neat intro - anecdote • good examples from past • ending - strong	• punctuating dialogue • paragraphing
Kate P.	• image-making details • strong, effective dialogue - shows personality • lead grabs interest	• edit out parts that don't relate to story

Noting Students' Strengths and Needs

At the start of the year, I create two kinds of record-keeping sheets that I use to jot down key strengths and needs of students as I read pieces. Since completing this form takes time, my goal is to take detailed notes once every six weeks.

An error tally (next page) is another record-keeping strategy that keeps me attuned to students' needs. As I read their pieces, I tally errors such as run-on sentences, too many commas, and mispunctuated dialogue. Then, to help me organize students for mini-lessons, I jot down on another sheet of paper students' initials next to the appropriate number. The list guides my decisions on which mini-lessons would benefit students' writing and helps me group students for instruction.

Mini-Lesson Tally for Grade Eight

1. Run ons, clause commas—20
2. Paragraphing—5
3. Colon—2
4. Commas—2

Students' Initials

1. JB, BF, PG, BL, SS, LT, LG, JM, TD, PD, CB, DM, CP, MS, RC, RD, MM, AR, JT
2. RG, CM, CR, TH, JT
3. BL, SS
4. JB, CM, LT, TD

Usually, I do a tally like the above example. Every six weeks, if there's time, I take notes on individual students (see page 14).

Challenge: *How would you prioritize this list and organize mini-lessons?*

These forms give me the mini-lesson topics I need to present to the entire class, individuals, or small groups. Equally important, completing these forms builds my background knowledge about each student's writing strengths and areas I believe the student can improve. Acquiring background knowledge on each student informs the questions I pose and the suggestions I offer during mini-conferences.

Mini-conference with Juanita, a sixth grader

TOPIC: End-of-sentence punctuation

Robb: The description of your room makes me feel as if I'm there. There are so many details. Read the first few lines aloud. [Juanita reads.] Can you tell me why you haven't marked the ends of any sentences?

Juanita: [Long pause before she answers.] I'm never sure how to do this. I usually put in too many periods, so now I don't do it.

Robb: Let's work on a few lines together and talk about where to put punctuation and why that's the best place. [At this point, I spend five minutes with Juanita, but I know that we will have to work on understanding what makes a complete sentence.]

My Observation

Though Juanita can show details, her writing is difficult for peers to read because she omits punctuation and paragraphing, and jumbles the speakers of dialogue. I chose working on punctuating sentences because I believe that once Juanita can successfully mark sentences, then we can move to punctuating dialogue and separating paragraphs.

Juanita does not understand the elements of a complete sentence, and when she punctuates, it's based on guesses. I schedule several ten-minute conferences with her and buddy Juanita with Lindy, who can offer peer support when I'm not available.

Note that with both José and Juanita, I open with positives. This is crucial. Young writers, like all writers, are fragile and need to know what they did well before addressing revision and editing.

Whole-Class Strategy Lessons

Based on the tally on page 15, I would repeat strategy lessons on repairing run-ons and punctuating compound sentences. *Three times in one week* I repeat this lesson for the entire class and circulate among students, helping them repair sentences in their second drafts and other pieces.

Small-Group Strategy Lessons

With a small group I review punctuating clauses and prepositional phrases that open a sentence. Other students are working on writing. On other days, I give strategy lessons to the five students who need to work on paragraphing and the two students who need to learn when to use a colon. Scaffolding occurs in small groups where I circulate among students, helping each one apply strategies for deciding when to start a new paragraph.

One-to-One Mini-Conferences

I hold five-minute mini-conferences on commas with each student. Using my own writing, I first think aloud to make my process visible. Then I model how I discover missing commas.

You will continually monitor students' needs all year, for they will change as students grow and improve and show you, through their writing, what they have learned.

Is There a Sequence for Teaching Grammar and Punctuation?

"What grammar should I teach and when should I teach it?" is a question teachers frequently pose. There's no prescribed order for mini-lessons in the middle grades. My notes from reading students' work and my observations from mini-conferences that I hold during writing workshop enable me to organize students for the grammar and punctuation instruction they need to improve their writing.

In grades four to six, I introduce the colon and semi-colon and various clauses only to students who can handle these topics. With younger students, I work a great deal on specific nouns and strong verbs, pronouns, paragraphing, commas, forming possessives, repairing run-ons and fragments, and the active voice.

To help students vary sentence openings in these grades, I avoid naming clauses and provide them with an "Idea Box" of words and phrases they can use to avoid starting sentences with the same word (see pages 58 and 68 and my book, *Brighten Up Boring Beginnings and Other Quick Writing Lessons*).

Again, the most effective way to discover students' needs is reading their work. When students' writing features errors such as run-on sentences and sentence fragments, it's time to celebrate. Errors instruct teachers, pointing out that students are experimenting with language and are ready to listen to mini-lessons and apply what they've learned to their writing (Graves 1994; Weaver 1996; Atwell 1999).

Each year, I chronicle the sequence of my grammar, usage, and punctuation teaching in a small notebook. Though I always start with parts of speech so students can create strong, clear images, I find that I'm always weaving in topics that respond to students' errors. And the nature of students' errors differs from grade to grade and year to year. I thought it would be helpful for you to see my school-year log that reveals how I depart from the traditional sequence of topics and which topics I frequently repeat. (See next page.) Note that some lessons are whole group but more are small group and individuals.

Grammar and Punctuation Lesson Log
Eighth Grade: 1999-2000

September
nouns
verbs
active voice
editing symbols
graphic cues

October
verbs, review nouns
active voice
adjectives
fragment repairs
editing symbols

November
run-on repairs
paragraphing
pronoun references
nouns, possession
graphic cues

December
pronouns & sent. variety
active voice
ways to vary sentence
semi-colon or conjunction
combining sentences

January
capitalizing proper
nouns & adj.
combining sentences
fragment repairs
commas—overuse
pronoun reference

February
paragraphing
adverbs
commas
semi-colon
possessive nouns & pronouns

March
combining sentences
run-on repairs
prep phrases
clauses, use of
capitalizing proper nouns, adj.

April
phrases
active voice
colon
graphic cues
pronouns, sent. variety

May
pronoun reference
adverbs
clauses, use of openings
noun, verb review
possessive nouns, pronouns

June
review—student requests

Grammar Lessons and Strategies Scholastic Professional Books

Parts of Speech Create Strong, Specific Images

Actor Kenneth Branagh once said, "The more words one has, the more one begins to understand." Simple, but profound. Vocabulary shapes our thinking; words build our ability to comprehend. The first words toddlers speak as they learn language are nouns, naming words. Nouns name persons, places, living creatures, things, ideas, feelings, and so on. For some teachers, asking students to learn the definition of a noun is sufficient. For me, it is insufficient because memorizing an explanation does not ensure that students will search for specific nouns to make their writing clearer, more detailed, and therefore, more interesting.

Poet J. Patrick Lewis calls nouns the muscle of writing, and an overload of adjectives, the flab. Nouns that are specific re-create in the reader's mind images the writer sees. But students tend to write in generalities rather than specific details. Instead of *daffodil*, students write *flower*, instead of *firefly*, they write *bug*, instead of *popcorn*, they write *snack*.

I find that engaging students in experiences that expose them to ways writers use nouns raises students' awareness of the importance of nouns in writing and provides them with opportunities to learn from a wide range of models. Encourage students to tune in to nouns by inviting them to do the following.

Collect Nouns

Collect nouns and other parts of speech from newspapers and magazines, free reading books, poems by favorite authors, or conversations with friends.

During reading workshop, students can record these unusual words and phrases in personal notebooks. (I have students make 4- by 6-inch notebooks filled with unlined paper, with construction-paper covers.) Some teachers prefer simply to set aside a section in students' notebooks or response journals for collecting words.

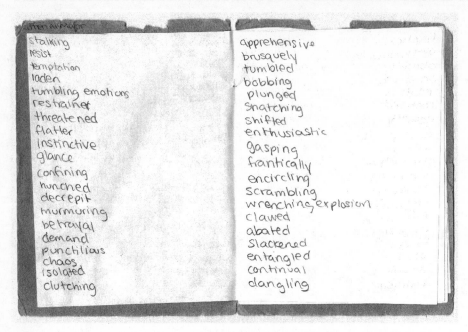

stalking
resist
temptation
laden
tumbling emotions
restrainer
threatened
flatter
instinctive
glance
confining
hunched
decrepit
murmuring
betrayal
demand
punctilious
chaos
isolated
clutching

apprehensive
brusquely
tumbled
bobbing
plunged
snatching
shifted
enthusiastic
gasping
frantically
encircling
scrambling
wrenching, explosion
clawed
abated
slackened
entangled
continual
dangling

I collect the notebooks daily and store them in a shoe box. If notebooks travel home with students, many forget to bring them back to school. Instead, when I want students to jot down words at home, I give them a sheet of paper that can be taped or stapled into their notebooks.

Eighth grader's word notebook

Introduce word-collecting notebooks

I introduce this collecting strategy with a think aloud, explaining how the strategy helps me:

> When I read poems, articles, the newspaper, and books, I keep a small notebook handy. Every time I read a noun that catches my attention, I jot it down. Before and during writing, I reread these lists to stimulate ideas in my mind and to search for a noun to replace one I've used. The lists are useful when I'm revising. Compiling lists is enjoyable because I learn so many new words—and words are a writer's business.

Next, I show students a recent notebook (see below), write some nouns on the chalkboard, and invite them to comment or pose questions.

Pages from Laura Robb's notebook

Nouns — heirloom, eccentrics
spinster
frugality heap
critters blades
fungi symphonies
crevices attar
intoxication tomb
alabaster chambers
scoundrel lutes
prosaic days covert
countenance legacy
amber smile
thunderbolt beggar
jasmines crumb

Verbs — jostle
swilled gnashed
grieved ebbs
fizzled botched
perched connive
swooped mired
radiate envisage
craned scrutinize
tatted walloped
tilt sputter
gloat slither
contorted fester
dwindled presage
burnished remedy
scudding licks
stooped drips

Grammar Lessons and Strategies Scholastic Professional Books

Students frequently ask, "Do I have to do this?" "Yes!" I reply. In my classes, everyone tries this strategy for six weeks. How can students determine whether a strategy supports their writing if they haven't used it and reflected on its benefits?

Ask students to share their collections with a partner, small group, or the entire class. Discuss whether they find the strategy useful and why or why not. After the trial period, if several students decide they don't want to continue using word-collecting notebooks, that's fine.

As students learn about other parts of speech, invite them to collect unusual or striking examples. I also encourage students to record phrases that interest them. For many students, these collections become valuable resources as they draft and revise. Often one word or phrase sparks an idea. Rita, a seventh grader, told me: "When I read the phrase 'comforting embrace' [from "Foster Home" by Nikki Grimes] the words 'cruel embrace' popped in my mind—just what I needed for my story."

Mine books and poems for specific nouns

Invite students to study and discuss how published writers effectively use nouns. In addition to their free-choice reading books, students can dip into picture books and poems, which are rich in specific nouns because authors of these genres must use words economically.

Two to three times a week, I invite students to select specific nouns from a text they are reading. For ten minutes or so, students read aloud their examples, while I record the nouns on chart paper. "Searching for specific nouns," a seventh grader told me, "helped me understand that terrific writers don't use words like *things* and *stuff*." The examples below are from sixth graders. I've underlined the nouns students shared.

> The <u>boughs</u> of the cherry trees met in an <u>arch</u> above Sanjo Avenue. Muna walked beneath the pale pink <u>arcade</u>. It was as though all the ugliness he had ever known was excluded from this <u>paradise</u>. Even the people he saw seemed clothed in a <u>glow</u> of <u>perfection</u>.
>
> — *The Sign of the Chrysanthemum* by Katherine Paterson

> On sad days,
> I remember
> that my place in <u>heaven</u> is rented
> and the <u>currency</u> demanded
> is not the <u>yen</u> or dollar,
> but my <u>essence</u>.
>
> — "Quilted Soul" by Sherley Jean-Pierre

Forge connections to students' own writing

While you deepen students' awareness of specific nouns through the work of published authors, help them focus on and improve the nouns in their own pieces. In grades four through six, I initiate this process by circling four to five nouns in a student's piece that need to be specific. Scaffold instruction for older students who can't pinpoint nouns in their writing by circling them.

Then I ask students to work in pairs for five to ten minutes, helping each other find alternative nouns and jotting these in the margin. Before letting students work alone on this activity, you may want to sit side by side with a student and watch him or her circle nouns, offering support when necessary. Such close monitoring lets you know when students can experience success on their own.

Once students can select nouns independently, I ask them to circle three to five they could improve, jot alternative nouns in the margin next to the circled word, and then circle their favorite choice.

TEN NOUN-RICH PICTURE BOOKS

I read aloud picture books, such as the titles below, and point out nouns that grab my attention. Students also have many opportunities to read picture books, searching for nouns that appeal to their sensibilities.

- *Black Cowboy Wild Horses: A True Story* by Julius Lester, illustrated by Jerry Pinkney, (Dial, 1998).

- *A Boy Named Giotto* by Paolo Guarnieri, pictures by Bimba Landmann (Farrar, Straus and Giroux, 1998).

- *Breakfast at Liberty Diner* by Daniel Kirk (Hyperion, 1997).

- *The City of Dragons* by Laurence Yep, illustrated by Jean and Mou-Sien Tseng (Scholastic, 1995).

- *Excalibur* by Hudson Talbot (Morrow, 1996).

- *Farolitos for Abuela* by Rudolfo Anaya, illustrated by Edward Gonzales (Hyperion, 1998).

- *Going Home* by Eve Bunting, illustrated by David Diaz (HarperCollins, 1996).

- *O'Sullivan Stew* by Hudson Talbot (Putnam, 1999).

- *Waiting for the Evening Star* by Rosemary Wells, illustrated by Susan Jeffers (Dial, 1993).

- *Wolves* by Seymour Simon (HarperCollins, 1993).

STRATEGY LESSON..

Noun Word Walls

Introduction

"How can *hardship* be a noun? It doesn't name a person, place, or thing," fifth-grader Josh asked, voicing a confusion typical of middle schoolers. Like Josh, many students this age readily grasp concrete nouns, but not abstract nouns. For Josh, "things" in the traditional definition of nouns meant concrete, nonliving items such as a pencil, rope, or marble.

To help these students, I teach them the suffixes that indicate abstract nouns and help them build nouns with these endings (see box on page 25). This work enlarges their range of unusual vocabulary to use in their writing, too. Making noun word walls is an effective way to give students practice identifying nouns, moving from general to specific nouns, and understanding abstract nouns.

Grade 8 Mini Word Wall	
Space Words + Phrases	
droid	heavens
rocket	jet plane
moons	space shuttle
galaxy	space food
light years	zero gravity
space odyssey	distant
evening star	explorers
meteors	revolve spheres
comets	pivot dazzled
robot	verify starstuff
black holes	energy
sun spots	weather
space suit-gear	close encounter
space/moon walks	buoyant
floating	marooned
weightless	halo
planets	spew
space photography	inferno
tele scope	luminescent
life in other galaxies	orbit
beaming pie	asteroids
untamed	atmosphere
remote control	density
universe	radiation

Eighth Grade Mini Word Wall

Grade 5 Mini-Word Wall	
Autumn Words + Phrases	
chill	un rippled
zephyr	rippled
bonfires	bare branches
bales of hay	dry bone wind
twirl, whirl	sunsets
leaves dance	apple picking
morning frost	pumpkin patches
dew	thunder bolt
illuminate	leathery bark
harvest moon	stubby bark
leap, bounce	splatters
crunching leaves	spurts
pumpkin fields - gold	
luminous	
silvery fingers	
leaves painted crimson and gold	
lily-gold moon	
raking leaves	
rustle	
brilliant maple	
jostle	
cloudburst	
torrent	
squall	

Fifth Grade Mini Word Wall

As a class, we spend two to four weeks adding nouns to a chart tacked to a bulletin board. I like to focus noun word walls on a specific topic, such as nouns that relate to autumn, holidays, space, friendship, vacations, adventures, birthdays, and so on. Students can fill charts with nouns throughout the year—just tack one over the other to save space.

Purpose

To help students understand that nouns are naming words; to sharpen students' awareness of general and specific, concrete, and abstract nouns; to collect nouns related to a theme; to enlarge students' vocabulary

Materials

Newspapers, magazines, books, poems, construction paper or large chart paper, marker pens

Suggestions

1   On the chalkboard, write general nouns such as *things, stuff, game, gift* and ask the class to brainstorm corresponding specific nouns. Fifth graders offered *kick the can* for *game,* and *magnifying glass* and *binoculars* for *stuff*.

2   Invite students to write—on Post-its or in their word-collecting notebooks— specific nouns from their reading, listening, and writing.

3   Collect the nouns and print them on construction paper or large chart paper. Display on a bulletin board or class wall.

4   Spend five to eight minutes a day collecting nouns from students. I like to have students print their words on the chart. Do this for two to four weeks, especially if students show they need additional experiences.

5   Encourage students to use the noun wall for their writing and spelling. Model this by using the noun wall as you demonstrate writing techniques and when you and students collaborate and compose in various genres.

   For example, sixth-grader Tamika decided to rewrite this sentence, filled with general nouns that I circled while sitting with her. The noun chart on birthdays offered ideas for her revisions.

Tamika's Original Sentence:

   At my party we had games, ate lots, and did fun things.

Tamika's Rewrite:

   At my birthday party, boys and girls did a balloon dance and played charades. Everyone ate pretzels, nachos and salsa, and chocolate cake with ice cream.

   "The chart on birthday words helped me," Tamika said at a mini-conference. "I needed two sentences because I wanted to be very specific. Jenna [Tamika's revising partner] said that my new sentences made her know what the party was like."

   Collecting nouns that relate to a topic before writing builds vocabulary and offers a wide range of choices as students plan and draft.

On Another Day

1 Introduce abstract and concrete nouns by creating a short list of each and asking students to categorize the list into two different columns. Here's the list I offer eighth graders: *ethics, lioness, resistance, computer, childhood, orphan, multitude.*

2 Follow steps 2 to 5 above, collecting and categorizing lists on concrete and abstract nouns.

On Another Day

1 Have students collect words related to a theme such as space, peer pressure, the environment, oceans, survival, and so on. Such lists not only activate and enlarge students' prior knowledge about a topic but also are top-notch resources for writing about these topics.

2 Follow steps 2 to 5, collecting themed lists.

SUFFIXES THAT BUILD ABSTRACT NOUNS

Here are suffixes that indicate a **condition, accomplishment,** or **state**:

Suffix	Example
-asm	enthusiasm
-ation	syncopation
-cy	occupancy
-dom	kingdom
-hood	adulthood
-ice	justice
-ics	ethics
-ings	earnings
-ism	realism
-itis	tonsilitis
-itude	aptitude
-ment	contentment
-ness	happiness
-osis	hypnosis
-red	kindred
-ship	friendship
-ty, ity	certainty, creativity

Here are suffixes that show a **belief** or **attitude**:

-ism	Shintoism
-ity	Christianity

Here are suffixes that indicate a **process** or **product**:

-age	marriage
-ion	action
-ism	hypnotism
-sion	confusion
-tion	rejection
-xion	reflexion

Adapt for Grades 4 and Up

Proper and Common Nouns

Introduction

The excerpt below, from a revised draft of Tony's memoir, indicates a need for this sixth grader to deepen his knowledge of proper nouns and develop his editing eye.

> Every summer we went to saranac, a lake sitting in the heart of the appalachian mountains. Just as the sun peers above the mountains, my dad, our neighbor mr. richards, and myself packed our backpacks with a days food and drink.

Tony is not alone. Many students compose early drafts that look like his. Though his writing is lovely, the student hasn't been able to edit for capital letters or other punctuation. "I don't see it," Tony tells me. First, through mini-lessons, I try to develop a keener understanding of the difference between common and proper nouns. To sharpen Tony's editing skills, I scaffold the process (see box on page 27). It takes several months of continual practice with editing cues before I invite Tony to work independently. Some students need more time and scaffolding to reach independence—two to three years. Rushing the process can escalate frustration and anxiety levels. Observe and communicate and students will show you when to nudge them to another level.

Purpose

To help students understand the difference between common and proper nouns and why proper nouns start with capital letters; to apply this knowledge to their writing

Materials

noun word wall, students' writing from their folders or journals

Suggestions

1 Write on the chalkboard some common and proper nouns, such as *ocean, Atlantic; city, Chicago; boy, Adam.*

2 Invite students to explain the difference between the words that start with lowercase letters and those that start with uppercase letters. A sixth grader said: "*ocean, city,* and *boy* are not exactly like *Atlantic, Chicago,* and *Adam.* A proper noun gets a capital letter because it names one boy, one ocean, and one city."

3 Have groups select several common nouns from the word wall and write corresponding proper nouns for each.

4 Ask students to search for common and proper nouns in the newspaper and in a book they are reading.

5 Have students share their findings with the entire class.

SCAFFOLD EDITING

Support students' editing by providing visual cues. The purpose of scaffolding is to empower students to become skillful editors. For students to improve, *they* have to edit, not the teacher. Here's what I do to call students' attention to editing needs:

1. Place a pencil check in the margin next to each line that needs editing.

2. Focus students on *one punctuation item* at a time. For Tony, it's looking for proper nouns and adding capital letters. Others might work on commas, apostrophes, run-on sentences, etc.

3. Sit side by side the first time and help the student slowly and carefully read each line, finding and completing corrections. You might have to do this several times.

4. Decide if it's time to turn some editing responsibility over to the student. Start the process by showing how you edit, and then have the student complete the editing independently.

5. Repeat step 3 several times, if necessary.

6. Add additional scaffolding to students' edited papers if they have not found everything by placing a check above the word or place that requires punctuation.

7. Continue scaffolding, gradually diminishing your support and moving students to independence. However, if students' pieces reveal that they continue to require support, provide it.

After reading Kaelyn's piece, I chose to have her focus on using commas. I placed check marks beside sentences involving commas to signal this.

STRATEGY LESSON ....

Revising Pieces for Specific Nouns

Introduction

"I'd rather do grammar exercises from a workbook than revise and edit my paper," a frustrated fifth grader admitted after his teacher and I presented a revision lesson.

When I asked Jamal why he felt that way, he said, "In my old school, I got all A's on the worksheets. The teacher corrected my writing. Doing my own [corrections] is hard." Students like Jamal can benefit from your support as well as from working with a peer who enjoys revising and editing and understands the process. I always honor students' feelings by saying, "It is tough to revise your own papers, but you are the writer and you need to make the choices" or "I understand how you feel and I'll help you until you're comfortable." Then slowly I nudge them forward.

Purpose

To enable students to apply their knowledge of specific and proper nouns to their writing

Materials

overhead transparency and projector, marker pens, students' writing folders

Suggestions

1 Place a section of a piece of your writing or a *former* student's writing on a transparency. If you use a student's work, don't identify the child.

2 Circle one to three general nouns.

3 Brainstorm, in the margin, specific nouns that might replace each circled noun.

4 Think aloud and show students your decision-making process as you choose the most effective noun.

5 Have students circle four to five general nouns in a piece of their writing. If students have difficulty identifying these, you circle them.

6 Ask students to brainstorm, in the margin next to the circled noun, several specific alternatives. For example, a fifth grader circled "lots of presents" in this sentence: I opened lots of presents at my birthday party. Her brainstorming of possible replacements for "lots of presents" also revealed her interest in art: *paints, charcoal, watercolor paper, inline skates, blue jeans, sweatshirt*.

7 Organize students into partners and have pairs add to each other's brainstormed mini-lists.

8 Ask students to revise the circled nouns by writing the new word above the circled one.

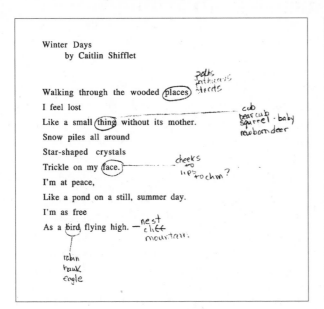

On Another Day: Link Proper Nouns to Students' Writing

Suggestions

1 Tell students to select an unedited piece of writing from their folders.

2 Invite students to proofread their writing and circle incorrectly punctuated proper nouns.

3 Using a different colored pencil or pen, have students correct by placing the editing symbol (see page 86) for capital letter under the first letter of each proper noun.

DECISION-MAKING SNAPSHOTS

When I introduce noun word walls and notebooks for collecting nouns and other parts of speech, I carefully observe students. Their level of understanding enables me to decide whether to move forward quickly or revisit abstract nouns. Some students arrive in my eighth-grade room with a solid knowledge of nouns. When that is the case, I quickly move students to improving their pieces by adding specific nouns and move on to verbs and using adjectives sparingly. Students' prior knowledge and experiences determine the pace I establish. Most often I group students: Those who can move on to studying another part of speech do, while a few meet with me two to three times a week for ten to fifteen minutes to deepen their understanding of nouns and learn to identify nouns in their own writing.

A point comes, however, when I must move on, even though one or several students might still have difficulty selecting nouns from their writing or finding nouns during a book or magazine search. During the year, I review topics (see schedule on page 18), providing students with more chances to comprehend and apply a concept.

STRATEGY LESSON..

Grab Your Audience With Strong Verbs

Introduction

When I introduce the term "strong verbs," my eighth graders grin and ask me, "How can a verb be strong?" True, strong verbs don't have the quality of physical strength that bodybuilders possess. Instead, strong verbs have the power to capture imagined action and construct sensory pictures that enable the reader and the writer to envision similar images (Graves 1994; Noden 1999).

To create an awareness of the power of strong verbs, place a section of a novel or poem on an overhead transparency. Show students how you underline the strong verbs and think aloud, telling them the image one or two of the verbs conjure in your mind. Then invite them to think aloud, sharing images they see. Here's the think aloud I presented to sixth graders using this passage from Natalie Babbit's *The Eyes of the Amaryllis*:

> *It seemed as if she'd only dozed a moment before she woke to hear Gran calling her. "Geneva! Get up! High tide." Dazed, she tumbled out of bed, found her shoes, pulled them on without thinking, and shrugged into her dressing gown. Downstairs, Gran waited at the door, a lantern dangling from one hand, the other gripping her crutch.*

Robb's Think Aloud for *dozed*:

> <u>Dozed</u> creates a picture in my mind of Geneva nodding off. Her mind won't let Geneva travel into a deep sleep because she might not hear Gran's call.

Suggestions for Student Practice

Once you've modeled selecting strong verbs and thinking aloud, invite students to work with a partner or in a small group, share a verb and the sentence it's in from their free-choice reading book, and then think aloud for the group. As students work, circulate, assisting those who struggle with finding verbs in a sentence. This kind of practice can improve students' ability to identify verbs, and it raises their awareness of how writers create pictures with verbs.

Sixth-grader Anthony's Think Aloud for *stumbled*:

> The word <u>stumbled</u> made me see Geneva getting out without thinking of what she was doing. She stumbles because she's already thinking of dressing and meeting Gran. It also shows that she was sleepy and not all awake.

Sixth-grader Yolande's Think Aloud for *shrugged*:

> I kinda saw Geneva get into her dressing gown in one motion—like you shrug your shoulders. I thought <u>shrugged</u> gave the dressing a fast feeling and one without thinking, like the way she did her shoes.

TEN BOOKS THAT ILLUSTRATE STRONG VERBS

Select passages with strong verbs from books to share and discuss with students. Also invite students to search for image-making verbs by asking pairs to read picture books, magazine articles, or their own books and share these in groups or with the entire class. Here are ten titles I often use:

◎ *Alvin Ailey* by Andrea Davis Pinkney, illustrated by Brian Pinkney (Hyperion, 1995).

◎ *Call Me Ahnighito* by Pam Conrad, illustrated by Richard Egielski (HarperCollins, 1995).

◎ *Chrysanthemum* by Kevin Henkes (Greenwillow, 1991).

◎ *How Turtle's Back Was Cracked: A Traditional Cherokee Tale* retold by Gayle Ross, paintings by Murv Jacob (Dial, 1995).

◎ *JAZPER* by Richard Egielski (HarperCollins, 1998).

◎ *Night Sounds, Morning Colors* by Rosemary Wells, illustrated by David McPhail (Dial, 1994).

◎ *Rattlesnake Dance* by Jim Arnofsky (Putnam, 2000).

◎ *Swine Lake* by James Marshall, illustrated by Maurice Sendak (HarperCollins, 1999).

◎ *William Shakespeare and the Globe* by Aliki (HarperCollins, 1999).

◎ *Zeke Pippin* by William Steig (HarperCollins, 1994).

Adapt for Grades 4 and Up

STRATEGY LESSON...

Spotlight Strong Verbs on Word Walls

Introduction

Verb word walls can tune students in to the rich amount of words in our language that have similar meanings. Instead of using the verb *walk* to describe how a character moved, I want students to refine the image and search for a verb that accurately shows the walk. *Trudge, stroll*, and *limp* are stronger and can better portray the action.

Build verb walls throughout the year by including strong verbs that can be used when writing about:

◎ holidays and birthdays

◎ themes the class is studying, such as space, friendship, conflict, peer pressure, weather

◎ the seasons

◎ similar words for *walk, said, cried, talked*

◎ sports

◎ dance, singing, acting, music

If you have limited wall space on which to hang large pieces of construction paper, use a wide roll of adding-machine tape. Attach strips of adding-machine paper to a wall or bulletin board and record verbs. It's easy to change these. Just roll up and store ones you've completed, making room for new lists.

Purpose

To help students explore verb possibilities and choose the one that creates the strongest image; to generate lists of strong verbs students can refer to as they draft and revise

Materials

books, magazines, poems, chart paper and/or adding-machine tape, marker pens

Suggestions

1 Help students understand that in a sentence, verbs show what happens and how it happens. Stronger, more colorful verbs, such as *sizzle*, appeal to our senses, enabling readers to picture, taste, feel, hear, and smell.

2 Write, on an overhead transparency or chart paper, sentences with weak and strong verbs. Here are two pairs of sentences I share with fifth graders:

> Molly went to the store.
> Molly skipped and jogged to the store.
>
> The third graders go into the gym.
> Third graders charged into the gym.

3 Involve students by asking: "How did your sensory images change when you read the second example? What other verbs might work? Why?"

4 Invite students to collect strong verbs from their reading and write these on the verb wall. Spend six to ten minutes three to four times a week gathering students' examples. Continue collecting over several weeks or collect intensively for two weeks. As you review verbs, have students add to the lists.

5 Focus verb lists on writing topics, units of study, or synonyms.

6 Encourage students to use these lists as they draft and revise pieces.

7 Create a list of verbs and other words to avoid in writing—words that don't create images. I call these "banished words" (see next page).

SIXTH GRADE'S LISTS OF STRONG VERBS

Instead of "go," try:	Instead of "fall," try:
walk	tumble
ride	twirl
trudge	whirl
amble	plunge
depart	glide
disappear	descend
recede	collapse
travel	swoop
journey	plummet
creep	rain
crawl	slip
run	sink
dash	topple
flow	founder
roam	cascade
drag	parachute
hike	submerge
march	coast
parade	
saunter	
stroll	
stride	
meander	

List of Banished Words

During the year, students and I create a list of words—various parts of speech—to avoid in their writing. I start the list, and in a think aloud, I explain the rationale behind it. Students enjoy bringing candidates before the class, and everyone votes to see which words make the list. I tell them, "This year we'll work together to cull words to avoid in writing. Words on the list are ordinary and don't appeal to the senses. The list will help you eliminate these words when revising."

Here are some of the words that made it onto my eighth graders' list:

a lot	get	make	went	pretty	good
bad	beautiful	go	come	nice	fun
cute	okay	say	do	stuff	things

STRATEGY LESSON...

Appreciate Poets' Use of Strong Verbs

Introduction

Like Louise Rosenblatt (1978), I believe that students should respond to literature aesthetically and emotionally, before we invite them to analyze structural elements such as meter, figurative language, strong verbs, or specific nouns. Doing this allows readers to enter the heart of the writing.

This may be especially true for reading poetry. When you offer pairs or groups of students poems to read, first invite them to read out loud and listen to the poem. Then have them discuss their reactions, raise questions, and reflect on the way the poem speaks to them. Students enjoy reading aloud and sharing their discoveries with classmates, and this affords everyone an opportunity to hear many poems and become familiar with the condensed language of poetry.

Each year, I add poems to file folders, expanding my collection. I find poems in anthologies, magazines, and collections by favorite poets. As students browse through these poetry resources, they discover poems they want classmates to read.

Purpose

To illustrate how poets use strong verbs; to discuss how sensory-rich verbs affect readers

Materials

poems, collections and anthologies of poetry

Suggestions

1 Select two to three poems with image-making verbs. I use two poems by Emily Dickinson that groups of students have read aloud many times and discussed.

2 Organize students into groups of three to five.

3 Ask students to reread their poem and discuss Dickinson's use of strong verbs.

4 Have students underline the verbs they thought were strong.

5 Invite students to take turns thinking aloud, explaining why the noun or verb helped the poet effectively paint a picture or arouse the senses (see pages 30 and 35).

6 Repeat this strategy lesson, focusing on or reviewing specific nouns.

Two Poems by Emily Dickinson

The wind begun to rock the grass
With threatening tunes and low—
He <u>flung</u> a menace at the earth—
A menace at the sky.

The leaves <u>unhooked</u> themselves from trees—
And started all abroad
The dust <u>did scoop</u> itself like hands
And threw away the road.

The wagons <u>quickened</u> on the streets,
The thunder <u>hurried</u> slow—
The lightning showed a yellow beak
And then a livid claw.

The birds put up the bars to nests—
The cattle <u>fled</u> to barns—
There came one drop of giant rain
And then as if the hands

That held the dams had parted hold
The waters <u>wrecked</u> the sky
But overlooked my father's house—
Just quartering a tree.

She <u>sweeps</u> with many-colored brooms—
And leaves the shreds behind—
Oh, housewife in the evening west—
Come back, and <u>dust</u> the pond!

You dropped a purple raveling in—
You dropped an amber thread—
And now you've <u>littered</u> all the East
With duds of emerald!

And still, she <u>plies</u> her spotted brooms,
And still the aprons fly,
Till brooms <u>fade</u> softly into stars—
And then I come away—

Seventh grader's Think Aloud

I think that the verb <u>flung</u> followed by the noun <u>menace</u> work together in this first stanza. <u>Menace</u> is a great way to say a threat, and using <u>flung</u> shows the wind's anger as it starts a storm. And then before the rain and lightning and thunder, you know a storm is coming because the sky looks threatening and the earth darkens. With a verb and noun, she created a story in my mind.

Eighth grader's Think Aloud

It took me many readings and lots of talk with my group to figure out that this poem was about sunset. The verbs <u>sweeps</u>, <u>littered</u>, <u>dust</u> are all about making things dirty and cleaning. It's cool how the clear sky of day is made dirty with different colors and then it all goes away into evening and stars. <u>Fade</u> is the verb she uses to show this. It's also a more gentle verb than <u>litter</u> and <u>sweep</u>. I think the verbs helped me see the changes at sunset. Jeremy said that <u>housewife</u> was a great noun because it set up a metaphor of a housewife who didn't clean her rooms, but littered the sky with colors and then cleaned them up into evening.

Offering students such experiences with poetry, where they dig their way into the meaning and the structure, is an exciting collaborative literary experience. It also can raise students' awareness of the following:

- the language of poetry
- vocabulary
- specific nouns
- shaping a poem
- stanzas, rhyme, rhythm
- poets' use of punctuation
- function of verbs

STRATEGY LESSON...

Revising Pieces for Strong Verbs

Introduction

A sixth grader began her short narrative this way:

Every Saterday I get to go with my dad. We go to the park. It's fun.

In a mini-conference, I helped Janetta circle "get to go" and "go" and suggested that she could improve these verbs. Then I asked her questions to generate more detailed language: "What time does your dad arrive? Does your dad drive? Walk? Take a train or bus? Is the park far away? What do you do that's so much fun?"

As she spoke, I jotted her responses on Post-its. Her speech contained rich details: "I'm looking out the window watching Dad park his old Chevy convertible and I hear his footsteps on the stairs and I'm waitin' at the door, happy he's come. We walk to the park—it's down the block—and Dad watches me swing and I pretend I touch the sky."

"Wow!" I exclaim, my immediate, honest reaction to Janetta's outpouring. First, I help her brainstorm and jot in the margin possible verbs and phrases, reminding Janetta of some she used while talking: *look, watch, listen, hear, charge, run, dash, walk, swing, touch the sky, make believe, pretend, dream.*

Next, I invite her to compose the first sentence out loud, and I write it for her. Janetta says it's easier to talk—writing it is hard. I want her to understand how her talk can be transformed into energetic writing. Here's her rewrite, which she completed during two workshops.

Evry Saterday I'm looking out the living room window waiting for dad. A horn toots. I think, thats him. He parks the old green car, charges up the stairs and sees me grining at the door. We dash down the steps and walk to the park near the house. I charge to the emty swing. Dad follows and pushez me higher and hiher until I feel like I can tuch the sky.

Not only did Janetta use strong verbs to breathe life into her piece, but she also added important details. "The questions helped me," she said. Editing will come later. Content is what's important now. My goal is for Janetta and other students to realize that writers ask questions—they probe and probe until they know what details to include.

When young writers revise their own work, they need time, support from a teacher, and strategies, like posing questions on Post-its, that generate more ideas than they need.

Purpose

To help students identify and revise colorless verbs in their writing

Materials

a piece of each student's own writing (poem or short narrative or essay)

Suggestions

1 Ask students to work in pairs and help each other circle three to five verbs they would like to improve.

2 Circulate and support students who have difficulty identifying verbs.

3 Have pairs brainstorm a mini-list of alternative verbs in the margin, next to the circled verb. Generating four to six verbs offers the author choices and creates an awareness of the range of possibilities.

4 Encourage the writer to read the sentence with each verb and select the best one. An eighth grader had this line in a poem: "My foot hit the soccer ball." Alternatives he listed for *hit* were *kicked, slammed, fought, banged, surprised*. He chose *surprised* because, "I wanted you [the reader] to feel the shock of the huge kick. My partner gave me that one—it was a great idea because in the next line I say, 'And like a cheetah, it flashed across the field.'"

5 Invite young authors to select a stronger verb to replace a circled verb by placing one line through the original verb and writing the new one above it.

6 Ask students to read their revised pieces aloud to their partners. Students sit side by side so they can see the original piece and the revisions.

7 Encourage partners to offer feedback about the revisions.

8 Move around the room and observe pairs as they work; listen to their conversations and ask questions to guide them.

9 Repeat activity on another day with different partners. You may find, however, that some students will integrate this strategy into their writing process immediately and want to work independently. I find that students in

grades five and six need to support one another for four to six months before they start to generate lists of words on their own. Struggling readers and writers in upper grades also require partner support, for their vocabulary is limited and generating word lists is difficult.

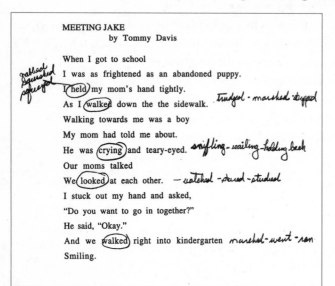

An eighth grader and I brainstorm vivid verbs before typing a final version of his poem.

To Use or Not to Use the Thesaurus

Some students turn to the thesaurus to discover words. The thesaurus is an excellent tool, however, often it is misused by students.

Too many students use the thesaurus to create a long list of alternative words. They copy every word without reflecting on whether a word fits the context of their piece or whether they truly understand its meaning. For some students, the thesaurus is a resource for finding words that will impress the teacher and their peers. Often, they plug in a word that makes no sense. Look at fifth-grader John's before and after sentences:

Before: My pony and I won the race.

After: My pony and I vanquished the race.

To avoid nonreflective use of the thesaurus, I tell students to include me in a thesaurus search. Meanwhile, I continually model how the thesaurus is an effective tool for discovering alternative verbs, nouns, and adjectives. Modeling includes how I find a word, focusing on the correct part of speech, and considering the choices, selecting words I understand and words that will work in my piece.

Young writers need to apprentice with an expert in order to learn to use this excellent word-finding tool. Experts can be older students, a peer, and the teacher. Whether searching for alternative nouns, verbs, or adjectives, teachers can prevent the pitfalls of exploring the thesaurus by thinking aloud to illustrate how we explore words.

STRATEGY LESSON...
Effectively Using Descriptive Adjectives

Introduction

Writers understand that adjectives, when used sparingly, can deepen an image or sensory response. Recently, I overheard a group of fourth-grade teachers discussing how they were focusing on students' writing with "plenty of adjectives so their pieces have descriptive details." Alas, what can happen is that students compose sentences that are laden with adjectives and that do more telling than showing. Fifth-grader Jeremy wrote: "We climbed that hot, scary, fearful stairway and found ourselves in a cold, frightening, ugly room." Clearly, Jeremy told readers to feel scared, frightened. Better to *show* details that let the reader conclude the experience was frightening.

Here's Jeremy's rewrite: "We climbed the stairs, suffocating from the hot air and landed in a room that felt like a deep freeze. Stiff mice dangled from the ceiling by their tails; icy green mold painted the wooden walls." The adjectives *hot, stiff, deep, icy, green,* and *wooden* clarified the image without telling the reader how to feel.

Purpose

To observe how published authors use adjectives; to help students select adjectives from their reading that clarify nouns and show, not tell

Materials

picture and/or chapter books, poems, chart paper, markers

Suggestions

1 Write, on chart paper, two to three examples of authors using adjectives that show, not tell. Here are two that I share with students:

> Murky water, slime-covered walls, dank and fetid air...Yes! Lucky me. The sewers of Paris!
>
> —*I Crocodile* by Fred Marcellino

> Sonny Greer pounded out the bang of jump-rope feet on the street with his snare drum. A subway beat on his bass drum. A sassy ride on his cymbal.
>
> —*Duke Ellington* by Andrea Davis Pinkney

2 I think aloud, referring to the first example: "The underlined adjectives show that the sewers were dirty, damp, with smelly air. But Marcellino never uses these "telling" words.

3 Ask pairs or small groups to discuss the second example. Here are some comments from eighth graders:

"The adjectives showed us the rhythms like <u>subway</u> and <u>jump-rope.</u>"

"And <u>snare</u> showed the kind of drum—that's important."

"I liked <u>sassy</u> 'cause it showed how the cymbals stood out."

I point out to students that they each used the word *show*. Then I ask them what feelings this passage stirred. "A hopping, jiving, showy drummer," Rick said. "And Pinkney didn't ever tell that."

On Another Day

1 Tune students' ears to the effective use of descriptive adjectives by asking them to study how their favorite authors and poets incorporate these in their writing.

2 Reserve three ten- to fifteen-minute sessions a week for two weeks for students to find and share examples from their reading.

3 Observe students' responses to this experience to decide whether to lengthen or shorten these adjective searches. Here are the examples shared by three seventh graders during their author study of Katherine Paterson's books:

Gilly grabbed the back of the striped pajamas with both hands and half dragged, half supported the faltering frame toward the couch.
— *The Great Gilly Hopkins*

I lured those fool cats right to me and into those infernal sacks.
— *Jacob Have I Loved*

His stare traveled from her filthy straw-sandaled feet to her cracked and frostbitten hands to her dry and lusterless hair to her brown face cut in quarters by a streaked white scar.
— *Of Nightingales That Weep*

Following are the students' comments:

Gina: She [Paterson] selects adjectives that paint clear pictures, like <u>filthy</u>, <u>straw-sandaled</u>, <u>lusterless</u>, <u>streaked</u>, <u>white</u> as a contrast to brown. She's showing how Takiko's looks changed, but she never says that she's now ugly—she leaves that thought to Hideo and the reader.

Marina: Her adjectives make you stop and want to reread—like <u>faltering</u> <u>frame</u> to show us how sick the huge Trotter is.

Marta: The adjective <u>fool</u> lets you know what Wheeze thinks of the cats, and <u>infernal</u> shows her attitude toward the sacks.

Once students have studied how professional writers use adjectives, invite them to select a piece of their own writing and change telling adjectives to ones that show.

Grammar Lessons and Strategies Scholastic Professional Books

Adjectives That Show

Introduction

The fifth-grade sample that follows illustrates how overused descriptive adjectives such as *pretty* and *beautiful* can weaken a piece.

> My room is pretty and beautiful. Soft, frilly, baby pink curtains are on the windows. There is a soft, comfortable, deep rose rug next to my bed. My best and favorite stuffed animals are on my toy chest. A tall bookcase is between the windows.

The adjectives tell the reader what to think and feel, instead of showing and permitting the reader to explore his or her own feelings and images. Now look at the rewrite, which the class and I wrote collaboratively on chart paper.

> In my room, I feel as if I'm wrapped in pink cotton candy. Next to my four-poster bed is a plush, rose-colored rug for relaxing and daydreaming. Pink curtains cover two windows and turn the sun's rays into pink sunbeams. Between the windows stands a tall and narrow bookcase that my grandfather made. My stuffed bear, lamb, bunny, and dog rest on a wooden toy box that looks like an old treasure chest.

The rewrite illustrates how strong verbs (*wrapped, daydream, stands*) and careful choice of specific adjectives (*plush, four-poster, tall, narrow, old, treasure*) improved the description. Adding similes also helped the reader come closer to the author's feelings about her room.

The process asks students to combine several writing techniques: selecting the right adjective; showing, not telling; and pinpointing places in their own pieces that need revision. To accomplish all this takes time. Therefore, revisit this mini-lesson many times and know that over several grades, most students will come to understand how to use adjectives to clarify images.

Purpose

To enable young writers to add specific adjectives to their own writing; to encourage economy when using adjectives

Materials

Students select a piece of their own writing, or the teacher can select pieces he or she knows would benefit from this kind of revision

Suggestions

1 Organize students into partners.

2 Have each student circle two to four nouns and/or descriptive adjectives. Circle the words for students who need additional support.

3 Invite partners to help each other generate a mini-list of possible adjectives to add to nouns or to replace the adjectives in their pieces.

4 Have partners choose the adjectives each considers most effective and read the piece out loud to each other, listening for sound, imagery, and meaning. One eighth grader added *weathered* to *barn*, another changed *crinkled* ear to *cauliflower* ear.

5 Collect examples from students and record on chart paper or the chalkboard.

6 Ask the class to discuss the effectiveness of these changes.

Pronoun Problems

Memorizing the various pronouns in the English language and searching for them in workbook sentences is not difficult for most students. I want students to be familiar with pronouns (see box, page 46), however, memory alone will not solve pronoun problems that teachers observe in students' writing.

As soon as I see students start a paragraph with a pronoun, use a plural pronoun to refer back to a singular subject, open a sentence with "Him and me" or "My sister and her" or "It was them," I launch into a series of mini-lessons that spotlight the pronoun misuse and have students spend time editing their own pieces.

DECISION-MAKING SNAPSHOT

For students to progress with revision and editing, they must be in charge of these events. Both in presentations and in published work, writing-workshop researchers Nancie Atwell and Lucy Calkins have cautioned teachers not take the pen from a student during a conference to demonstrate a revision or editing technique. Several years ago, I heard Nancie Atwell retract this position at a Virginia State Reading Association Conference—and the audience of several hundred teachers breathed a collective sigh of relief.

There are times when it's quite effective to show a student in a mini-conference how to rewrite a sentence or phrase, providing you think aloud as you rewrite, so students understand your reasoning.

"I needed to see what it looked like when you brainstormed a list of verbs" and "It helped when I saw how you looked for faulty pronouns usage" are comments that tell me some students need to work closely with the teacher to get it. Chart and chalkboard are too far away. Follow your teaching instincts and scaffold instruction as long as students require that level of support. Gradually diminish support as students progress.

Adapt for Grades 4 and Up

Pronoun References

Introduction

A <u>person</u> cannot walk away from a mandatory job feeling that <u>they</u> helped <u>their</u> community because <u>they</u> had no choice.

If each <u>one</u> has free time after school, <u>they</u> should be able to decide how to use that time.

Both sentences are from the second draft of an eighth grader's persuasive essay against an optional community-service policy at Powhatan School that the administration encourages students to complete before graduation. Using a plural pronoun to refer back to a singular subject and starting a paragraph with a pronoun are common errors among middle school students.

With the strategy lesson that follows, you can tune students' ears to pronoun usage issues. Present one issue at a time—too much information can daunt and confuse students who are unlearning speaking and writing patterns they've continually used.

Purpose

To create an awareness of pronoun reference issues; to help students understand the importance of these issues; to provide opportunities for students to correct their own work

Materials

chart paper, marker pens, students' writing

Suggestions

1 Record, on chart paper, errors students have made in previous years without identifying the students.

2 Here are the samples I prepare on the chart:

My brother broke his leg and they went to the hospital.
(grade 6)

The convertible and sports car raced down the highway and it won.
(grade 7)

3 Think aloud and explain why the pronouns confuse. Here's what I say:

Both sentences have pronoun reference problems. This means the pronouns used are confusing. In the first sentence, the subject, <u>brother</u>, is singular, but the pronoun is <u>they</u>. The author wrote <u>they</u> because his parents drove to the hospital. This sentence doesn't make that clear. In the second sentence, two cars race, but the pronoun <u>it</u> doesn't help me know which car won. I'm sure the author knew which was the winner, but it's important to help readers understand.

4 Ask students to work in pairs and rewrite the sentences. Here are seventh graders' revisions:

My brother broke his leg and my parents drove him to the hospital. The convertible and sports car raced down the highway and the sports car won.

5 Repeat steps 3 and 4 two to four times or until all or most students can revise the samples you present.

6 Give students a piece of their writing with pronoun reference issues. Place a check in the margin next to the line that has the error and have them rewrite on a Post-it or a piece of scrap paper.

7 Ask students who don't have any corrections to support a classmate or to continue working on a piece of writing.

8 Scaffold instruction for students who need more support (see page 27).

On Another Day

1 On chart paper, write an example of faulty pronoun use when starting a new paragraph. Here's what I print:

My uncle honked the horn as he parked his white sedan in front of the house. Immediately, my brother and I jumped off the stone stoop and climbed into the back seat. Uncle Dave drove to the amusement park, and my brother and me counted the money mom had stuffed into our wallets.

He thought the day was perfect for it and we were excited. (grade 8)

2 Think aloud, showing students how confusing it is to open a paragraph with pronouns. Here's what I say:

The introduction is a grabber. Strong verbs <u>honked</u>, <u>jumped</u>, <u>climbed</u>, and <u>stuffed</u>. Starting the second paragraph with three pronouns that refer back to the first paragraph confuses. Who is the he? Uncle Dave, one of the brothers? What does "it" refer to? Does "we" mean all three? When starting a new paragraph, it's helpful to the reader to use names instead of pronouns.

3 Follow steps 5 through 8 from the previous lesson.

Adapt for Grades 4 and Up

Using Subject Pronouns

Introduction

Changing speech patterns that students constantly hear at home and in their community is challenging. Such change takes consistent scaffolding over several years, for the grammar pattern has been programmed in students' memories since early childhood.

When students say, "Him and her went to the movies" or " It was him who won the game," I repeat their sentence using correct English. My goal is for them to hear correct English many times. To provide models for students, I construct a "Help Chart," post it on a bulletin board, and leave it there as a reference throughout the year.

Purpose

To help students understand that subject pronouns open a sentence and are used after *is* and *was*

Materials

chart paper, marker pens, students' own work

> **HELP CHART**
>
> **Start sentences this way:**
> He and I...
> She and I...
> Mother and I...
> Jane and...
> She and Mother...
> He and Jane...
> Mark, Jill, and I...
>
> **After *is* and *was*, use subject pronouns:**
> It was I...
> It was he...
> It was she...
> It is they...
> It is he...
> It is she...
> It is I...
> That's she...

Suggestions

1 On chart paper, write examples of errors students have made in previous years, without identifying the students. For example:

> Her and me played on the swings.
> Me and Tony rode horses.

2 Here's how I think aloud:

> If you open a sentence with pronouns, they are the subject of the sentence, and that is why writers use the subject form of pronouns. Open the first sentence with "She and I" and the second sentence with "Tony and I."

3 Ask students to work in pairs and rewrite several sample sentences (you can write these on chart paper or give them to students as handouts).

4 Repeat practice two to four times or until all or most students can revise.

5 Give students a piece of their writing. Place a check in the margin next to the line that has the error and have students rewrite on a Post-it or a piece of scrap paper.

6 Ask students who don't have any corrections to support a classmate or to continue working on their writing.

7 Scaffold instruction for students who need more support (see page 27).

On Another Day

1 Write more sample sentences on chart paper. For example:

It was them knocking at the door.
That's him playing in the yard.

2 Think aloud and include these ideas:

The samples above are incorrect in written English but over time have become common in spoken English. Use subject personal pronouns after the expressions "It was…, It is…, That's…." The correct form sounds wrong to many of you because you are not accustomed to hearing it in conversations.

3 Repeat steps 4 through 7 from the above lesson.

PRONOUN RESOURCE BOX

It's important for students to be familiar with pronouns. Such familiarity gives us a common language, making it easier for me to model, think aloud, and discuss. I share the following list with students:

Personal Subject Pronouns: I, you, he, she, it, we, you they

Personal Object Pronouns: me, you, him, her, it, us, you, them

Personal Possessive Pronouns: my, mine, your, yours, his, her, hers, its, our, ours, your, yours, their, theirs

Reflexive: myself, yourself, himself, herself, itself, ourselves, yourselves, themselves

Demonstrative: this, that, these, those

Indefinite: all, both, each, some, several, one, few, many, either, neither, every, none, any, most, everyone, someone, anyone, everybody, someone, somebody, nobody

Relative: who, which, that, whose, whom

Interrogative: who, which, what, whose, whom

Displaying and Storing Strategy Lesson Charts

Hang strategy lesson charts on a wall or bulletin board so students can refer to them. If I'm presenting three strategy lessons on pronouns, I display all three for students to use. If wall space is tight, tape one in front of the other or attach each chart to coat hanger and place one behind the other so students can flip to the chart they need.

Store strategy lessons on skirt hangers and hang on a wall hook or in a closet. When you review a topic, such as adverbs, reuse the mini-lesson(s) and display to refresh students' memories.

Understanding Adverbs

"Adverbs are easy," an eighth grader tells me. "They all end in *ly*." Year after year this explanation resurfaces when I invite students to tell me what they know about adverbs. Adverb word walls quickly dispel this myth and enable students to revise their thinking about these words and discuss how adverbs can clarify meaning in a sentence. "By the end of the week, as we [the class] reread the lists of adverbs, I finally believed that there were lots that didn't end in *ly*," a sixth grader said. "Now I can see how adverbs work."

Adapt for Grades 4 and Up

STRATEGY LESSON ....

Adverb Word Wall

Introduction

Like adjectives, adverbs modify other words, and they modify verbs more often than they modify adjectives or other adverbs. It's easy to detect adverbs because they usually answer these questions: *When? Where? How? How much?* or *How long?*

Building a word wall of adverbs like the one shown on the next page will help deepen your students' understanding of this part of speech.

Purpose

To see that many adverbs don't end in *ly*; to understand that adverbs answer specific questions

Materials

chart paper, marker pens

Suggestions

1 Make four headings on chart paper: *Where? When? How? How much?/How long?*

2 Spend five to ten minutes a day for four days collecting words from students that fit each category. Most *ly* words will fall under *How?*

3 Check, in the dictionary, any words you or your students challenge.

Where?	When?	How?	To What Extent?	
here	then	endlessly	never	possibly
there	often	quietly	very	away
inside	soon	softly	far	not
outside	later	rather	almost	
up	today	quite	too	
down	tomorrow	smoothly	also	
nearby, near	always	intently	somewhat	
far	now			
	daily			
	yesterday			

Adapt for Grades 4 and Up

STRATEGY LESSON..

Adverbs Can Clarify Meaning

Introduction

Because adverbs can make a place more specific (We played *outside*), make time more accurate (I'll meet you *tomorrow* morning), and describe how (the motor purred *smoothly*), they can clarify meaning, an image, and sensory experiences.

Used sparingly, adverbs enhance writing. Students always agree that the adverb *very* is overused and they add it to the list of "Banished Words" (see page 33).

Purpose

To show students how adverbs can improve writing

Materials

chart paper, marker pens, students' own writing

Suggestions

1 On chart paper, write sample sentences without adverbs. Here's what I offer students:

> **The twins pedal their bikes.**
> **The Smiths moved.**

2 Invite students to select adverbs to add to each sentence. Here's a sixth grader's rewrites:

> **The twins pedal their bikes quite rapidly.**
>
> **Yesterday, the Smiths carefully moved furniture from room to room.**

3 Ask students to discuss how the adverbs affect meaning. One sixth grader noted, "The Smith sentences had different meanings—in one they moved out of their house, in the other they moved furniture around in the same house."

4 Have students rewrite simple sentences for two to four days or until you observe that they understand the concept.

On Another Day

1 Ask students to select a piece of their writing.

2 Help them find a place in their piece where they can add or adjust adverbs to clarify meaning.

3 Scaffold students who still don't have the hang of using adverbs by selecting a sentence or short passage from their writing and having them revise it. Go over their work in a conference; share how and why you might tweak the adverbs.

Does Teacher Support Always Equal Student Progress?

Even though you offer students individual support several times a week, they might not progress at the rate you have planned. Years of writing and speaking incorrectly combined with a lifetime of hearing incorrect grammar from peers or others can deeply entrench poor habits. Continue scaffolding instruction for these students and know that they'll need many years of support to undo ingrained speech and writing patterns.

As you introduce a part of speech and focus on it, many students will connect collaborative practice during mini-lessons to their own work. Even though students gain proficiency using their knowledge of the parts of speech to improve writing, it's difficult for them to integrate revising for verbs, nouns, adjectives, and pronouns at the same time.

I find that I work on one item at a time with my writing. If you want students to complete multiple revisions, set up guidelines like these:

1 Circle three to four nouns that you can make more specific.

2 Circle three to four verbs that could be stronger.

3 Reread your piece to check for pronoun references.

Focusing on one element at a time ensures more success for students and can lessen frustration and anxiety.

Part II

Improving Sentence Structure

O n a cool September evening, I sat at our dining room table. A stack of first drafts sixth graders had turned in that day waited for me. A warm fire blazed close by, and as I settled into the task, I wondered what I would learn about my students' writing. As I read, I jotted down observations on a dated sheet of paper. I noted run-on sentences, a lack of paragraphing, and misuse of commas. Virtually every student needed to improve sentence structure. I made a summary note to present mini-lessons on varying sentence openings, clarifying details, and adding specific details.

The following day, I presented a mini-lesson on varying sentence openings. From there, I broke the class into small groups and gave them sample sentences to rewrite. Students who got it then applied this skill to their own pieces. Students who needed more guidance worked in pairs or with me. This process—model, practice, release to independence—informs most of my teaching and is certainly mirrored in the structure of the strategy lessons in this book. I move students from daily practice, which enables them to gain insight into a strategy, to applying the strategy to their own writing. How do I know that it's time to invite students to rewrite parts of their own pieces independently? When they can explain a strategy and successfully complete practice exercises.

Can Understanding Participles Improve Style?

It's difficult to figure out just how to begin teaching students to improve sentence structure. There are certain parts of speech—participles, absolutes, and appositives—that, once mastered, go a long way toward improving writing (Noden 1999). So in this section of the book, I'll show you how I teach prepositional, infinitive, and participial phrases; clauses, appositive, and absolutes. The background information I've included is primarily for you, the teacher. You, in turn, can share it with students as you present mini-lessons. In these lessons (see first one, on page 58) you'll notice that I simplify definitions or skip them altogether. So for each lesson—which is more like an artist's sketch than a completed painting—you will need to explain background and model. Then invite students to analyze examples, find examples from their books, choose words and phrases from the Idea Boxes, and practice the grammar strategy. Once older students gain competency in applying a technique to their own writing, teachers can expand definitions. From my experiences with students in grades four through nine, this occurs with many students in grades eight and nine and with some students in grade seven.

Background Information

Prepositional Phrases

With a prepositional phrase, writers can vary sentence openings and use the phrase to show the relationship of a noun or pronoun to another word in the sentence. A prepositional phrase starts with a preposition and ends with a noun or pronoun, called the object of the preposition.

Used to vary sentence openings:

Before: A gift is under the bed.
After: Under the bed is a gift.

Used to show relationships:

The gift <u>under the bed</u> is for Mom.
The gift <u>on the bed</u> is for Mom.
The gift <u>near the bed</u> is for Mom.

PREPOSITION RESOURCE BOX

On a sheet of paper, I write the prepositions, subordinating conjunctions, and relative pronouns, making copies for each student to put in his or her writing folder. You may also want to print these words on a chart and display it.

Prepositions

aboard	among	between	from	over	underneath
about	around	beyond	in	past	until
above	at	but (except)	into	since	unto
across	before	by	like	through	up
after	behind	down	near	throughout	upon
against	below	during	of	to	with
along	beneath	except	off	toward	within
amid	beside	for	on	under	without

Compound Prepositions

because of	according to	in spite of
on account of	instead of	out of

Grammar Lessons and Strategies Scholastic Professional Books

Notice that each preposition changes the relationship between the gift and the bed.

Participles

A participle is a form of a verb that's used as an adjective. Two kinds of participles function as adjectives: the present participle that ends in *-ing*, and the past participle that usually ends in *-ed*, *-d*, or *-n*. Used alone, participles can vary sentence openings as well as modify nouns or pronouns within sentences.

> **Before:** The broken goggles became foggy under water.
> **After:** <u>Broken</u>, the goggles became foggy under water.

> **Before:** The stampeding horses were frightened and passed the noisy crowd.
> **After:** <u>Stampeding</u>, the frightened horses passed the noisy crowd.

Participial Phrases

Often a participal introduces a group of related words that function as an adjective. This group of words, called a participial phrase, can vary sentence openings and add details to nouns and pronouns within sentences.

Used to vary sentences:

> **Before:** I sat in front of the control panel of the spaceship, and I pressed a lever that ignited the rockets.
> **After:** Sitting in front of the spaceship's control panel, I pressed the lever that ignited the rockets.

Used to add details within a sentence:

> **Before:** The aliens were bewildered by their image in the clear pond.
> **After:** The aliens, bewildered by their image in the clear pond, kept staring at themselves.

> Note that the participial phrase eliminates the passive voice—"were bewildered"—and makes it active—"bewildered."

Dangling Participles

Participial phrases are said to "dangle" when the phrase that opens a sentence does not modify the noun or pronoun that follows.

Dangling Participle: Shouting wildly, the horses chased the crooks.

Corrected: Shouting wildly, the crooks ran from the posse chasing them on horseback.

Gerund Phrase: A gerund is the present participle form of a verb and ends in *-ing*. A gerund phrase includes the gerund and all words related to it; it's an effective way to vary the openings of sentences.

Used to vary sentence openings:

Before: The purpose of the coach shouting was to get the team to understand the next play.
After: <u>Shouting at the team</u>, the coach hoped they would understand the next play.

Infinitive Phrases

An infinitive is the present tense of a verb preceded by *to*: *to run, to jump, to fly*. The infinitive becomes a phrase when other words modify the verb form: *to run around the track, to jump over the stream, to fly in a balloon*. Infinitive phrases can vary sentence openings.

Used to vary sentence openings:

Before: You bear right at the fork in the road and you'll come to the river.
After: To reach the river, bear right at the fork in the road.

Subordinate Clauses

A subordinate clause cannot stand alone because it does not express a complete thought. Subordinate clauses that start with subordinating conjunctions function as adverbs and are an effective way to vary sentence openings and add details within sentences.

PUNCTUATION TIP

When a clause opens a sentence, set it off with a comma.

Used to vary sentence openings:

Before: The roller coaster ride was so fast we were frightened.
After: <u>Because the roller coaster ride was so fast</u>, we were frightened.

Used to add details in a sentence:

Before: We worked on the house and rested.
After: We painted the house and, <u>when we were totally tired</u>, we rested.

SUBORDINATING CONJUNCTIONS

after	as long as	before	so that	until	wherever
although	as soon as	if	than	when	while
as	as though	in order that	though	whenever	
as if	because	since	unless	where	

Adjective Clauses

A subordinate clause that functions as an adjective modifies a noun or pronoun. A relative pronoun introduces most adjective clauses. The adjective clause usually follows immediately after the noun or pronoun it modifies. Adjective clauses improve writing because they add details to a noun or pronoun and clarify meaning in a sentence.

Before: That student, James, is remarkable.
After: James is a remarkable student <u>who overcame blindness and graduated from high school with honors</u>.

Noun Clauses

Clauses that act like nouns in a sentence are called noun clauses. The focus here is on noun clauses that function as the subject of the sentence because these can be used to vary sentence openings. Subject noun clauses usually begin with *that, whatever, whoever, what.*

Examples:
>That the coach hollered showed his frustration.
>What you decide to do will affect the rest of the family.
>Whatever the package contained is not your concern.
>Whoever erased the math problem needs to rewrite it.

Absolutes

In his book, *Image Grammar*, Harry Noden defines the absolute as a noun combined with the present participle of a verb (*-ing* ending) or the past participle (*-ed,-d,* or *-n* ending). Examples of absolutes are *jaws cracking, hands disfigured, body shivering.* Absolute phrases are an effective way to open sentences; they are also powerful to include within a sentence to add action to an image and show details instead of telling.

Used to vary sentence openings:
>**Before:** The gymnast was nervous as he approached the parallel bars.
>**After:** Hands shaking, feet trembling, the gymnast approached the parallel bars.

Used within sentences:
>**Before:** The cat was ready to pounce on the mouse.
>**After:** The cat, teeth bared and legs stretching, eyed the mouse.

Appositives

An appositive is a noun that adds another image to a preceding noun. Appositives improve writing because they expand details and paint clearer images in the reader's imagination.
>**Before:** The vulture eats dead animals.
>**After:** The vulture, a scavenger, eats dead animals.

Appositive Phrases

Writers can create appositive phrases by adding more details to the appositive.
>**Before:** The vulture, a scavenger, eats dead animals.
>**After:** The vulture, a scavenger that flies over roads and meadows, eats carrion, or dead animals.

Clause or Phrase?

A clause has a subject and a verb. A phrase does not have a subject and a verb.

PUNCTUATION TIP

Set off an *appositive* or *appositive phrase* by placing a comma before and after the phrase.

When an absolute starts a sentence, place a comma after the participle. When an absolute interrupts a sentence, place a comma before and after it.

In the section that follows, I offer guidelines for presenting mini-lessons that use this complex background information to show young writers how to improve their sentence structure. I also include practice exercises for students to complete after your mini-lesson but before they move to revising their own pieces.

Tips for Presenting the Mini-Lessons

The suggestions that follow can strengthen your presentation of the mini-lessons in Parts II and III of this book.

1 Make a transparency of each ready-to-use mini-lesson.

2 Use a blank sheet of paper to cover parts of the transparency you are not discussing.

3 Start by reading aloud the title and purpose to students.

4 Read the **Literary Example** and discuss it with students. Encourage them to find examples to bring to the class the next day, from fiction, nonfiction, and poetry they are reading. Studying examples from literature reinforces the connection between learning grammar and improving writing.

5 Read the **Before Example**. Ask students what they notice about the writing. Ask questions such as: "Is anything repeated? Is any part unclear or confusing?" Compare it to the literary example.

6 Think aloud and point out what you believe needs revising.

7 Uncover the **Idea, Brainstorm,** or **Help Box** and the **After Example**. Read the revised example.

8 Stimulate discussion with the **Get Students Involved** section. Use whatever time remains for students' input and questions.

9 Return to the **Get Students Involved** section on another day; you'll need ten to fifteen minutes to complete this. Have small groups or pairs of students rewrite the **Before Example**. Compare completed work to the **After Example** on the transparency and invite students to choose the most effective writing and offer reasons.

10 After the mini-lesson, leave the transparency on the overhead so students can use its tips, words, and phrases to guide their practice exercises and rewrites.

11 After presenting the mini-lesson, store the transparency in a file folder so students who need to review the lesson can revisit it by themselves or with your support.

12 Use a water-soluble pen to write students' comments and suggestions on a transparency. With a damp tissue or paper towel, wipe off the comments and reuse the mini-lesson.

13 Write the mini-lesson on large chart paper if your school does not have an overhead projector. Review and revisit as needed.

Tips for Evaluating the Activities

Here are some suggestions that can make each writing exercise a valuable assessment and evaluation tool.

◎ It's not necessary to grade writing exercises. Read them quickly to see which students understood and internalized the mini-lesson and which students would benefit from repeating the mini-lesson and an additional practice exercise.

◎ Students who need additional practice can complete the second writing exercise, labeled "A."

◎ If students demonstrate that they get it after completing the first exercise, ask them to select a piece of writing from their folder to improve, applying the strategy or strategies they've practiced. With some students, you might have to select pieces and mark places that need revision.

◎ You can pair students who understand the mini-lessons with those who need extra practice. This frees you to work individually with those students who need scaffolding.

◎ Once students can apply a writing strategy or technique, have them include it in their writing folders on a list titled "Things I Can Do." Students can review the list prior to editing a first draft and set individual goals.

STRENGTHEN WEAK WRITING

As your students learn to use clauses and phrases, appositives and absolutes, they will eliminate these writing pitfalls characteristic of middle grade and middle school writers:

◎ starting several consecutive sentences with the same word or phrases

◎ telling readers what to think and how to feel

◎ writing in general rather than specific terms

◎ cluttering sentences with unclear ideas

---

1 Spice Up Sentence Beginnings With Prepositional Phrases

PURPOSE: To show students how prepositional phrases can vary consecutive sentences that start with the same word

Before Example

The dwarves covered their faces with black masks. The masks looked like vulture heads and had sharp beaks. The dwarves rode into the forest on ponies as dark as midnight and were dressed in black suits. The leader whooped and whistled and charged ahead, and the other dwarves answered with bold war screams.

Revision Tips

1 Put a check next to sentences that start the same way.

2 Rewrite. Try starting sentences with a prepositional phrase. Choose from the prepositions in the Idea Box.

3 You might add or omit some words from each sentence.

4 You might combine two sentences into one.

5 Read your revised paragraph and listen for the difference!

After Example

On the dwarves' faces were black masks that looked like vultures with sharp beaks. In black suits and riding ponies as dark as midnight, the dwarves rode quickly toward the forest. Throughout the charge toward the forest, the leader whooped and whistled, and the other dwarves answered with bold war screams.

Get Students Involved

ASK: "What did you learn from the Literary Examples? How did the After Example improve the paragraph? Are there other rewrites you prefer?" Explain why.

Literary Examples

On Monday mornings we built a fire under the iron pot in which we boiled the bed clothes, work clothes, and linen.
— Mildred Pitts Walter, *Second Daughter: The Story of a Slave Girl*

At the last station the deacon and his wife had given them a heavy blanket and an oilskin tarp.
— Kathryn Lasky, *True North: A Novel of the Underground Railroad*

IDEA BOX

	against	below	during	near	over	toward
across	at	beyond	for	off	since	under
amid	around	by	in	on	throughout	up
after	behind	down	into	onto	to	with

Student Practice 1

DIRECTIONS: Rewrite the paragraphs below.

The dragon guarded a treasure of jewels and gold in the Cave of Winter. The elves lived above the dragon's cave at the foothills of Avalanche Mountain. The dragon had three heads and two whipping tails attached to its scaly body. The elves wanted some of the treasure in spite of the dangers of battling the dragon.

REWRITE: _____

_____

_____

_____

_____

_____

_____

Student Practice 1A

The last avalanche piled snow over the homes of the elves. The snow froze many elves inside their homes. And some elves who were away from the foothills held a long meeting about purchasing new and safer land. And before dawn, the remaining elves marched toward the dragon's cave. And the elves threw poison spears onto the dragon's head and body and the dragon closed its eyes and slept.

REWRITE: _____

_____

_____

_____

_____

_____

_____

2 Put a New Spin on Openings With Participial Phrases

PURPOSE: To show students that verbs that end in *-ing*, *-ed*, *-d* or *-n* are participles and can be used to introduce a participial phrase; to show how these phrases enliven paragraphs by varying a repetitive subject-verb pattern of sentence beginnings

Literary Examples

cascading over the asphalt village

breaking against the black sky over 1-2-5 street

— Walter Dean Myers, *Harlem*

Raising his arms, Rabbi Loew chanted zirufim, mighty spells from Cabala.

— David Wisniewski, *Golem*

Before Examples

1 The man in the black cape took off the hood and revealed his skull-like face.

2 The gnarled old woman snapped her fingers and muttered an incantation, then transformed into a fish, a swan, and an eagle.

3 The puppy barked and scratched because he was in a locked trunk.

Revision Tips

1 Reread the sentence.

2 Find a section that can be changed into a participial phrase.

3 Brainstorm possible participial phrases.

4 Move the participial phrase to the front of the sentence.

5 Set the phrase off from the rest of the sentence with a comma.

6 Add or delete words to craft your sentence.

After Examples

1 Wearing a black cape, the man ripped off the hood and revealed his skull-like face.

2 Snapping her fingers and muttering an incantation, the gnarled old woman transformed into a fish, then a swan, and finally an eagle.

3 Locked in the trunk, the puppy howled and scratched.

BRAINSTORM BOX

1. wearing a black cape, sporting a black cape

2. snapping her fingers, clapping her hands

3. locked in the trunk, bolted in the trunk

Get Students Involved

ASK: "Can you find examples of participial phrases in your free-choice reading books? Can you write other participial phrases for these sentences? How does beginning a sentence with a participial phrase improve the sentence?"

Student Practice 2

DIRECTIONS: Choose three participial phrases from the list below and craft sentences using the phrase at the beginning. Remember to set the introductory phrase off with a comma.

- Locked in the basement
- Destined for adventure
- Hanging from a tree's limb
- Driven to intense anger
- Looking through the mirror
- Frightened by the storm

_____

_____

_____

_____

_____

_____

Student Practice 2A

DIRECTIONS: Rewrite these sentences, opening each with a participial phrase. Remember to set the introductory phrase off with a comma.

1 We were standing on the dock and saw a boat sink.

2 Our car's front tire was punctured by a long nail.

3 Dad was costumed in a space suit and looked like an evil alien.

REWRITE: _____

_____

_____

_____

_____

_____

_____

3 Pick a Participial Phrase From Within a Sentence

PURPOSE: To show students that participial phrases within a sentence can be moved to the beginning of the sentence to eliminate repeated sentence openings; to show students that they can rewrite part of a sentence as an introductory participial phrase

Before Example . . . .

The gray clouds were gathering into a whirling mass. The gray clouds twisted into a funnel shape, raging across the sky. The farmer's house was shuddering in the high winds, for it was controlled by the elongated funnel cloud. The house was tossed through the air and landed on top of an old oak tree.

Revision Tips . . . .

1 Put a check next to sentences that start the same way.

2 Underline a participial phrase or a part of the sentence that can be changed into a participial phrase.

3 Rewrite by using the participial phrase to open the sentence.

4 You might add or omit some words from each sentence.

5 You might combine two sentences into one.

6 Read your revisions and listen to the change from passive to active voice.

After Example . . . .

Gathering into a whirling mass, the gray clouds twisted into a funnel shape and raged across the sky. Shuddering from the high winds, the farmer's house lifted off the ground, controlled by the elongated funnel cloud. Tossed through the air, the house landed on top of an old oak tree.

Get Students Involved . . . .

ASK: "Was the After Example an improvement? Why? Can you rewrite the paragraph using different participial phrases? Can you rewrite it so that only a couple of the sentences begin with participial phrases? Which rewrite do you prefer? Why?"

BRAINSTORM BOX

gathering into a whirling mass

shuddering from the high winds

tossed through the air

Student Practice 3

DIRECTIONS: Rewrite the paragraphs below so that each sentence begins with a participial phrase. Remember to set off each introductory phrase with a comma.

Janet found a secret passage exploring the old house. Janet lit a candle heading up the stairs to a bolted door. Janet jiggled the door's bolt and the door creaked open, flooding the hall with an eerie light. Janet stepped into a dimly lit room lined with wooden coffins.

REWRITE: _____

_____

_____

_____

_____

_____

_____

_____

Student Practice 3A

The tightrope walker was balancing on the high wire. The tightrope walker was performing leaps and somersaults high above the ground. The tightrope walker jumped to a nearby swing and entertained the crowd by standing on his head and catching tossed candy bars.

REWRITE: _____

_____

_____

_____

_____

_____

_____

_____

4 Catch Those Dangling Participles

PURPOSE: To alert students to the confusion created by opening a sentence with a participial phrase that is not connected to the noun or pronoun that follows the phrase; to show students that dangling participles can create sentences that don't make sense; to offer students suggestions for repairing dangling participles

Before Examples

1 Suffering from a twisted ankle, the race was lost by our track star.

2 After practicing the violin for hours, my recital for tonight was ready.

3 Locked in the closet, the meowing of our cat could be heard everywhere.

4 Caught in the storm, the side of the road was where the man pulled over.

Revision Tips

1 Place a check over the subject following the participial phrase.

2 Ask yourself, Does the subject relate to the phrase?

3 Find the word that the phrase modifies.

4 Rewrite the sentence, changing the subject so that the participial phrase modifies the subject.

5 Add or leave out some words as you rewrite.

After Examples

1 Suffering from a twisted ankle, our star track player lost the race.

2 After practicing the violin for hours, I was ready for tonight's recital.

3 Locked in the closet, our cat meowed so loudly we heard it everywhere.

4 Caught in the storm, the man pulled over and parked on the side of the road.

Get Students Involved

ASK: "What do dangling participles do to the meaning of a sentence? Can you add details to sentences to clarify ideas? How does this improve the sentence?"

Student Practice 4

DIRECTIONS: Identify the dangling participles and rewrite the sentences so the subject connects to the phrase.

1 Hanging from the ceiling, I watched the bat utter strange noises.

2 Canceled by two schools, we will play the soccer game tomorrow.

3 Filmed on several locations, the star of the movie was a gray dolphin.

REWRITE: _____

_____

_____

_____

_____

_____

_____

_____

Student Practice 4A

1 Coming in for a landing, the tower alerted the pilot of sudden wind gusts.

2 Broken into a dozen pieces, I saw my mom's vase on the floor.

3 Warped by the heat, my sister could not play her favorite record today.

REWRITE: _____

_____

_____

_____

_____

_____

_____

MINI-LESSON

5 Clarify Details With Subordinate Clauses

PURPOSE: To show students that subordinate clauses have subjects and verbs but they don't function as independent sentences or clauses; to show that these clauses can come at the beginning, in the middle, and at the end of sentences and add clarifying details

Literary Examples

When you go owling/you don't need words/or warm/or anything but hope.

— Jane Yolen, *Owl Moon*

They wanted each Birth mother to be assigned four births instead of three, so that the population would increase and there would be more Laborers available.

— Lois Lowry, *The Giver*

Before Examples

1 that Ann survived the accident

2 whatever the mechanic did to the motor

3 since the storm hit the town

4 what students painted during art class

Revision Tips

1 Find the subject and verb of each clause and notice that each clause cannot stand alone because it does not express a complete thought. All the Before Examples are sentence fragments.

2 Turn each clause into a complete sentence.

3 Place some clauses at the beginning, some in the middle, and some at the end of the sentence.

4 Try placing the same clause in two different positions.

After Examples

1 When we saw the demolished skis, we were thankful that Ann survived the accident.

1a That Ann survived the skiing accident is a credit to her training and physical strength.

2 Jane and I appreciated whatever the mechanic did to the motor, for we were able to drive to Las Vegas.

3 The entire town has been staying in the basement of the school since the storm hit.

3a The town seemed deserted since the storm hit, for everyone was in the basement of the school.

4 What students painted during art class, the teacher displayed in the school's library.

4a Parents enjoyed seeing what students painted during art class.

Get Students Involved

ASK: "Why are subordinate clauses fragments? Does the position of a clause change the meaning of a sentence? How do the clauses clarify meaning?"

Grammar Lessons and Strategies Scholastic Professional Books

Student Practice 5

Directions: Change the subordinate clauses, which are sentence fragments, to complete sentences.

1 whoever volunteered to baby-sit

2 until the boa constrictor is in its cage

3 that the gorilla is extremely unhappy

_____

_____

_____

_____

_____

_____

_____

_____

Student Practice 5A

1 as soon as the plane lands

2 whatever the team's captain promised

3 if snow falls this evening

_____

_____

_____

_____

_____

_____

_____

_____

MINI-LESSON

6 Capitalize on Clauses to Brighten Up Sentence Beginnings

PURPOSE: To teach students how to rewrite consecutive sentences that start with the same words; to show students how to vary the noun/verb pattern of sentences; to place a comma after an introductory clause

Literary Examples

Although we now know that the earth beneath us is not full of monsters, we still don't know very much about it.

— Peter Kent, *Hidden Under the Ground*

That had been some 20 years ago, and long after Bob left the Hunter Ranch, he found that everywhere he went he was known.

— Julius Lester, *Long Journey Home: Stories from Black History*

Before Example

Jamal stepped inside the haunted house. Jamal heard screams and groans. Jamal ran into the next room. Jamal saw himself in mirrors that lined the wall. Jamal's shape changed in each mirror.

Revision Tips

1 Put a check over sentences that start the same way.

2 Rewrite. Try starting sentences with words or phrases from the Idea Box.

3 Pull out a phrase from the middle of the sentence, start it with a word or phrase from the Idea Box, and use it for your opener.

4 Often you'll combine sentences.

5 You might add or delete some words.

6 Reread your revised paragraph and think about the difference.

After Example

As soon as Jamal stepped into the haunted house, he heard screams and groans. When Jamal ran into the next room, he saw himself in mirrors that lined the walls. Wherever Jamal looked, his shape changed.

Get Students Involved

ASK: "How did the rewrites in the After Example create more effective sentences? Can you craft other rewrites that are even better?"

IDEA BOX

	that	until	whoever	unless
as soon as	whatever	since	because	although
when	if	what	while	wherever

Student Practice 6

DIRECTIONS: Rewrite the paragraphs below so that the sentence openings vary.

   Tony sat at his desk in school. Tony was bored listening to the teacher drone on about the Boston Tea Party. Tony took out his cell phone and dialed the alien who lived with him. Tony whispered into the phone and asked the alien to make strange noises. Tony hid the cell phone in his desk. Tony and the class were startled by high-pitched screeches and groans. The teacher stopped lecturing and Tony was happy.

REWRITE: _____

_____

_____

_____

_____

_____

_____

_____

Student Practice 6A

   The girl on the train watched the other passengers. The girl took out her glass eye and brandished it in front of the people. The girl laughed when she saw the passengers cringe and look at their laps. The girl calmly popped the eye back in and walked off the train at the next stop.

REWRITE: _____

_____

_____

_____

_____

_____

_____

_____

7 Add Clauses Within Sentences for Clarity and Cadence

PURPOSE: To show that clauses within a sentence can clarify meaning by adding important details; to show that the details added by a clause create stronger images and provide more information

Literary Examples

Nathan began to breaststroke toward it, alongside Lighthouse George, who was keeping a close watch on him to see if he was as strong a swimmer as he'd claimed.
— Will Hobbs,
  Ghost Canoe

New scoundrels come in droves, illegally taking Mexican lands, until now there are tenfold more English-speaking Texans and loyal Spanish-speaking Mexicans.
— Sherry Garland,
  Voices of the Alamo

Before Examples

1 The astronaut trained.

2 Behind the tree lurked an alien.

3 A hairy tarantula crossed the road.

Revision Tips

1 Add clauses to the basic sentences.

2 Use words or phrases from the Idea Box to compose clauses that extend the basic sentences in the Before Examples.

3 Place the clause within each sentence you create.

After Examples

1 The astronaut trained <u>until every muscle in his body ached</u>.

2 Behind the tree lurked an alien <u>that had escaped from its spaceship after the ship landed</u>.

3 A hairy tarantula crossed the road <u>because it was searching for water</u>.

Get Students Involved

ASK: "What details did the clauses add? How did the details improve the sentences? Can you rewrite the Before Examples? Which rewrites did you like better? Why?"

IDEA BOX

	whatever	if	as long as
until	although	as soon as	unless
that	because	though	while
who	which	so that	wherever

Student Practice 7

DIRECTIONS: Rewrite the basic sentences, adding clauses within each sentence.

1 Flames jumped from house to house.

2 Black and menacing smoke surrounded the house.

3 The fire engines arrived.

REWRITE: _____

_____

_____

_____

_____

_____

_____

_____

Student Practice 7A

1 He dressed as a vampire.

2 White vampire teeth hung over his lips.

3 He hissed through his vampire teeth.

REWRITE: _____

_____

_____

_____

_____

_____

_____

_____

8 Accentuate the Appositives to Sharpen Images

PURPOSE: To help students understand that an appositive is a noun that adds details to a preceding noun; to show that an appositive can be enlarged into a phrase by adding more details

Literary Examples

EARTH-MOTHER,/
Mother of all our
brown-ness,/
Hands clasped with
arms/
stretching around the
world...
  — Margaret Walker,
      Mother of Brown-Ness

And Raven,/
Bold rascal Raven/
Cries River/
Slicing/
Stillness/
Winter ice.
  — Nancy White
      Carlstrom, *Raven
      Cries River*

Before Examples of Nouns Without Appositives

1 The <u>shark</u> swam near the surface.

2 The <u>criminal</u> was caught.

3 <u>Crows</u> are nature's cleaning service.

Revision Tips

1 Brainstorm other nouns and phrases that add details to the underlined word.

2 Rewrite the sentence using an appositive or appositive phrase.

3 Set off the start and end of the appositive or appositive phrase with commas when they interrupt a sentence. *Example:* The puppy, <u>a playful terrier</u>, will be Ricky's birthday gift.

After Examples

1 The shark, a predator seeking blood, swam near the surface.

2 The criminal, a bank robber, was caught.

3 Crows, carrion feeders, are nature's cleaning service.

Get Students Involved

ASK: "What images did the After Examples create in your imagination?" Try brainstorming other ideas for the Before Examples and rewriting each one. "Which appositives did you feel were stronger? Why?"

BRAINSTORM BOX

1. predator; predator seeking blood

2. a bank robber

3. carrion feeders; scavengers

Student Practice 8

DIRECTIONS: Rewrite the sentences below, adding an appositive or appositive phrase to the underlined noun. First jot down ideas in the Brainstorm Box.

BRAINSTORM BOX

1 <u>Tamika</u> is camping with us.

2 Don't lock the <u>door</u>.

3 My <u>sandwich</u> is delicious.

4 My mom reported the <u>noise</u>.

REWRITE: _____

_____

_____

_____

_____

_____

Student Practice 8A

BRAINSTORM BOX

1 The <u>dentist</u> was kind.

2 The <u>car</u> raced down the road.

3 The <u>snake</u> slithered through the meadow.

4 Yesterday, my <u>dog</u> ran away.

REWRITE: _____

_____

_____

_____

_____

_____

MINI-LESSON

9 Stir Readers' Imaginations With Absolutes

PURPOSE: To show that an absolute is a noun followed by the present (*-ing*) or past participle (usually ending in *-ed, -d, -n, -en*) of a verb; to enable writers to provide detailed images; to add action to a description

Before Examples

1 The cheetah attacked.

2 The squirrel skittered up the tree.

3 The driver passed the red convertible.

Revision Tips

1 Close your eyes and imagine an action for the underlined word.

2 Brainstorm possible ideas that start with a noun followed by a participle.

3 Rewrite, deciding the most effective place to add the absolute.

4 Place a comma after the absolute when it opens a sentence.

5 Place a comma before and after the absolute phrase when it interrupts a sentence. *Example:* The snake, <u>fangs bared and tongue flicking</u>, prepared to attack.

BRAINSTORM BOX

1. jaws opened, teeth bared, claws extended, muscles tensed

2. teeth chattering, body shivering, tail dragging

3. mind racing, upper body tensed, frustration developing, eyes narrowed

After Examples

1 Jaw opened and claws extended, the cheetah attacked.

2 The squirrel, body shivering, skittered up the tree.

3 Mind racing, frustration developing, the driver passed the red convertible.

Get Students Involved

ASK: "How did the absolutes improve the images and action of the After Examples?" Try brainstorming other ideas and improving the Before Examples. "Which do you like better? Why?"

Student Practice 9

DIRECTIONS: Add absolutes to each sentence. An absolute is a noun followed by a verb that ends in *-ing*, *-ed*, *-d*, or *-n*. Gather your ideas in the Brainstorm Box before revising.

BRAINSTORM BOX

1 The <u>ride</u> was scary.

2 We watched the <u>boxer</u> struggle.

3 Up the tree climbed the <u>cat</u>.

REWRITE: _____

_____

_____

_____

_____

_____

Student Practice 9A

BRAINSTORM BOX

1 The <u>scuba diver</u> approached the shark.

2 The <u>mummy</u> moved.

3 Slowly, the <u>boy</u> shape-shifted into a werewolf.

REWRITE: _____

_____

_____

_____

_____

_____

10 Combine Sentences With Conjunctions for Smoother Prose

PURPOSE: To show how the coordinating conjunctions (*and, but, for, nor, or, yet*) can be used to combine short, repetitive sentences into smooth-as-sea-glass prose

IDEA BOX

and
but
or
nor
for
yet

Before Example

Chris and I went fishing. We went fishing in the pond in Chris's cow pasture. We looked down as we walked. We looked down because we had to walk around dozens of cow piles. Chris disliked putting squirming worms on his fishing hook. He cast out. He cast out to the middle of the pond. He waited for a bass to bite. I cast out from the opposite bank. I cast out and waited and prayed for a big one.

Revision Tips

1 Underline repeated ideas that you can combine.

2 Rewrite by combining sentences and eliminating repeated ideas.

3 Use, if necessary, one of the coordinating conjunctions in the Idea Box to help you combine sentences.

4 Add or delete words to maintain clarity.

5 Read your new paragraph out loud and listen carefully, making sure that you've eliminated repetitions.

PUNCTUATION TIP

When you combine two sentences and each one has a subject, you've formed a compound sentence. Place a comma before the conjunction. **Example:** <u>Jim</u> rode his bicycle to the hobby shop, and <u>he</u> purchased a model race car to put together.

When you combine two sentences and drop the subject of the second, you don't need to place a comma before the conjunction. **Example:** My <u>brother</u> joined the swimming team and had to be at the pool by 6:00 A.M.

After Example

Chris and I went fishing in the pond in Chris's cow pasture. We looked down as we trudged across the field toward the pond, for we had to skirt around dozens of cow piles. Chris disliked the squirming worms, yet he baited his hook, cast out to the middle of the pond, and waited for a bass to bite. I baited my hook, but cast out from the opposite bank of the pond, and prayed for a big one.

Get Students Involved

ASK: "How did combining sentences improve the After Example?" (no repetitions, fluent, holds reader's interest, connects ideas that go together) "Did you notice any changes in verbs? Were these more effective? Can you rewrite the paragraph a different way?"

Student Practice 10

DIRECTIONS: Rewrite the paragraphs and eliminate repetitions. Use conjunctions to combine some of the sentences. You also can add stronger verbs.

John always felt a cold chill brush his face. The cold chill came in the darkness of night when John was in bed. The cold chill filled John with fear and tension. The chill kept John awake for hours. John wondered if he could discover what caused the icy breeze to visit him every night.

REWRITE: _____

_____

_____

_____

_____

_____

_____

Student Practice 10A

The beach was deserted. The beach was deserted because it was after midnight and all the bathers were asleep in their homes. A silvery shadow crept across the sand. The silvery shadow illuminated the crashing waves and the beach. The silvery shadow spotlighted a limp body washed onto the shore. The body crawled towards the dry sand. The silvery shadow followed it.

REWRITE: _____

_____

_____

_____

_____

_____

_____

Help Students Revise for Content

The "grammar work" I've outlined thus far can't be divorced from other revision strategies that are a part of the writing process. They are on a continuum. Once your students have gotten the hang of these several strategies for improving sentences, focus their attention on revising for content. To do this successfully, set specific revision guidelines that grow out of writing guidelines you establish with students. (When teachers tell students to rewrite and improve their piece without giving specifics, students flounder, because the nature of the revisions that the teacher wants is a mystery.)

In my eighth-grade class one January, students were working on writing memoirs. Before they began writing, they created content and editing guidelines with my help. These guidelines helped students as they draft, and become standards for revision and topics for revision strategy lessons.

Guidelines for Memoirs: Grade Eight

Content Guidelines

◎ Focus on one to two recollections.

◎ SHOW, don't TELL: offer rich details.

◎ Include dialogue and inner thoughts.

Editing Guidelines

◎ Punctuate quotations correctly.

◎ Show paragraphs.

◎ Use commas correctly with introductory clauses, appositives, absolutes.

While students' write their first drafts, I offer strategy lessons on punctuating quotations (see pages 90–91), when to start a new paragraph, and using commas. I make summaries of these lessons available on overhead transparencies or on chart paper as students edit. I repeat strategy lessons for students who need extra help. And I'm always modeling that the best way to edit is to focus on one guideline at a time.

Tips for Establishing Writing Guidelines

Throughout the year, I establish content and editing guidelines for free-choice writing and for pieces, such as the memoir, that everyone writes. At the start of the year, I include only two items under each category, because students and I have just begun to study strategies that improve content, punctuation, and usage. Content and editing guidelines grow out of the strategy lessons I'm presenting, and both of these often emerge from the needs students' writing shows me. My rule of thumb is no more than three to four content guidelines and two to four editing guidelines. Too many overwhelm and frustrate students, which defeats my goal of helping them improve.

Grammar Lessons and Strategies Scholastic Professional Books

When I sit side by side with a student, scaffolding the editing process, I use prompts and questions that I want students to internalize and use while they revise independently.

Prompts and Questions That Encourage Content Revision

- Have you read the piece out loud and listened for_____?

- Read the best part. Can you find another part that you could improve by bringing elements of the best part to it?

- Do you have details that don't relate to your topic?

- Do you have too few details?

- Does your lead grab the reader's attention? Should you write other leads?

- Is there more than one story in this piece?

- Are the details out of order?

- Where does the story take place? Is this clear to readers?

- Do sentences all begin the same way?

- Can you add appositives and/or absolutes to create stronger images?

- Are your ideas in a logical order?

- Have you sequenced the plot correctly?

- Are there repetitions that you can omit?

- Is the dialogue realistic?

- Does the ending grow out of the piece?

- Is the title short and snappy?

- Does the title reflect the content?

- Did you follow the content guidelines for this piece?

- Did you reread this draft to make sure you met the content guidelines?

If prompts relate to the focus of strategy lessons, then I post them on chart paper so students can refer to them as they revise. The more support you offer students, the better chance they have of understanding what Katherine Paterson says: *"I can't wait to finish my first draft, for then I can start revising and making it better. Revision is the only place in life where spilt milk can be turned into ice cream."* My goal is to help students understand that writing is revision.

Part III

Editing for Punctuation and Usage

"Me and Jim saw a movie this weekend." "Dantae seen a airplane yesterday." "Her and me baked a cake for my brother's birthday." "My dad tooken my sister to the movies."

These sentences, written by middle school students, illustrate syntactical patterns also evident in their speech. It is difficult to alter such speech and writing patterns in the course of one or two years. Here are some strategies that can support slow, continual change:

◎ When a student speaks incorrectly, rephrase what he or she says, using correct English. For example, if a student tells me, "Yesterday I swum across the pool," I respond with, "I'm glad you swam across the pool. Did you jump or dive in?" Instead of saying, "That's wrong," and wounding a student's self-confidence, it's kinder to repeat the sentence and allow the student to hear correct English usage. I always keep in mind that students' speech results from the patterns they've heard at home.

◎ Read aloud every day so students hear the rhythms and syntax of literary language.

◎ Demonstrate how students can edit their written work.

◎ Ask students to edit for one thing at a time; you may tell them to correct pronoun usage, place commas, or check for capital letters. It's difficult to integrate several editing standards and much easier to focus on one at a time.

◎ Provide students with revision checklists and individualize what you expect each child to accomplish.

◎ Work one on one or with groups of two to three students, first thinking aloud and modeling how you go about editing. Then scaffold the editing process with think alouds, prompts, and questions that can move students toward independence (see page 84).

Scaffolding in Action: Grade Eight

Background

Eighth-grader Patrick has highly developed speaking skills. He expresses ideas clearly, with details, and enjoys talking. Patrick struggles with writing, often overusing adjectives to "make it sound cool," opening consecutive sentences the same way, and including fragments and run-ons. Here is Patrick's first draft of a paragraph describing his room; the guidelines he wrote from are shown at left.

Content Guidelines

- Include specific details.
- Show how you use your room.
- Vary sentence openings.

Editing Guidelines

- Check for run-on sentences.
- Add comma after long opening phrase.

Patrick's First Draft

The light music absorbs your body while chilling on the beaming blue chair. The blending colors of the dark indigo couch and faint yellow chairs; pale white walls make you body and, mind relax. The faded out sounds of Moshi's tinkering collar around her neck, as she prances like a little kid into the mellow room. The musty carpet matches the large gray statue of a man, resting against the wall. The mantle piece is charcoal black from the hoping flames. The fire roaring on the large metal grill warms the room and gives and eerie feeling to the room.

First Scaffolding Conference: Ten minutes

The focus I give Patrick is to read his piece out loud and listen for consecutive sentences that start the same way. We review how phrases can introduce sentences, and I show Patrick how I pull out the phrase "resting against the wall." Patrick rewrites this sentence in front of me:

Resting against the wall is the statue of a gray man, the same gray as my musty carpet.

Patrick's First Rewrite

Light music absorbs your body while chilling out on the beaming blue chair. Colors of the dark indigo couch and pale yellow chairs blend; white walls make your body and mind relax. Prancing like a little kid into the mellow room, Moshi, my cat, tinkles the bells that hang from her collar. Resting against the wall is the statue of a gray man, the same gray as my musty carpet. The hopping flames have darkened the white mantle piece. The fire, hot and roaring warms the room and casts eerie shadows on the walls.

Second Scaffolding Conference: Eight minutes

Robb: You have repaired so many sentence openings—you're really making progress with that editing skill. I love the way you used phrases to vary those beginnings.

Patrick: Yeah, it's getting easier. But I still don't do it in first drafts.

Robb: That's difficult when you're concentrating on the content. That's what's so great about having chances to revise. Telling the reader that Moshi is a cat helped clarify that image. You changed hoping to hopping—all thoughtful edits.

Patrick: I got those from reading aloud. But I hate doing it—I feel so stupid reading out loud to myself.

Robb: I understand how you feel. But if the strategy helps, I say use it. You know, professional writers use it—reading aloud lets you hear what you've written. [Patrick nods.]
Whose room is this?

Patrick: Mine—that's obvious.

Robb: Reread and think about the pronouns you've used.

Patrick: Oh, I see—"your." [I nod.]

Robb: I'd like you to think of a lead that really grabs and lets the reader know you're in your room. Play around with that and note your revisions on the back of your paper.

Final Mini-Conference: Four minutes

A day or so later, Patrick and I meet. He shares his revisions. He's changed *your* to first person. Here's his lead and rewrites of the opening sentence.

Whenever I'm angry, I stomp into my room, slam the door shut, and feel the tension leave. Soft colors of the dark indigo couch and pale yellow chairs blend with the white walls, making my body relax and soothing my mind. I'm chilling out to the light music playing on my boom box. The bright blue chair absorbs my body.

After reading the revisions, I wrote these notes on a Post-it:

super topic sentence—ties all ideas together
I love the cause/effect setup
You've made great progress!

When I scaffold and confer with students, I use prompts and questions, such as "Whose room is this?" to turn the problem-solving process over to them. The prompts that follow can focus students on usage and punctuation issues. In addition to these prompts, you will develop questions from students' texts, just as I did with Patrick.

PROMPTS THAT FOCUS STUDENTS ON USAGE

- With direct quotations, do you start a new paragraph every time the speaker changes?

- Did you check punctuation for direct quotations against the samples on the chart?

- Are series of words set off with commas?

- Did you set off appositives and absolutes with commas?

- Have you used commas to set off items in dates and addresses?

- Have you used direct address? Did you correctly use commas?

- Do you have a comma separating two complete sentences joined by a conjunction?

- Have you paragraphed your piece?

- Have you used pronouns to start a paragraph? How can you repair this?

- Do you have end-of-sentence punctuation?

- Have you checked for capital letters?

- Have you mixed singular and plural pronouns?

- Have you mixed singular and plural subject and verb?

- Did you use semicolons correctly?

- Have you checked for nouns that show possession? Do you need an apostrophe?

- Have you used a colon? If so, correctly?

- Have you checked for run-on sentences?

- Have you edited for sentence fragments?

- Have you solved all the editing problems the margin checks indicated?

Improve Editing Skills and Sentence Structure

With the mini-lessons and practice pages in this section, students can learn to effectively use the following punctuation:

- forming the possessive case of nouns

- punctuating and setting up dialogue

- paragraphing

- placing commas

- using the semicolon and colon

Three mini-lessons will focus on fixing sentence-structure flaws that weaken a piece:

- sentence fragments that can confuse the writer's meaning

- jamming too many ideas into a sentence and creating a run-on sentence

- the passive voice

Mini-lessons in Part III follow the same format as those in Part II of this book. Review the "Tips for Presenting the Mini-Lessons" and the "Tips for Evaluating Activities" on pages 56–57 to refresh your memory.

Encourage Peer Editing

Once students understand the editing process and have spent several weeks practicing as I circulate around the room, I invite them to help each other edit. To make peer editing a successful experience, invite students to read their partner's work out loud from beginning to end, then reread to look for one editing issue. It's also crucial that the writer chooses an editing focus (see editing sheet on page 87 and Appendix A) so his partner knows what to concentrate on. Having the goal stated on the sheet also makes it easier for you to review students' work.

Peer editing is a helpful strategy, because students can pinpoint errors in others' writing much easier than in their own. Moreover, it saves you time and allows you to work with students who struggle with the process. When you pair students, make sure you team up students who are at similar skill levels, so they can support each other. Students who make abundant errors should work with you, for they require the kind of scaffolding that only a professional can offer

Teach Students Standard Editing Symbols

At the start of the year, I hand out to students a list of standard editing symbols (see next page) and suggest they paste it into their writer's notebook. I introduce students to these symbols so they can use them while they self-edit. If students can't locate a punctuation or usage error from my margin checks, then I write the appropriate editing symbol in the margin to make the clue more specific.

Review Mini-Lessons

Revisit the mini-lessons that follow many times, as some students will need extra modeling and practice before they can apply the knowledge to their own writing. Often, if students don't get it the first time around, I set the lesson aside, move on, and repeat the lesson several weeks later. Students' minds have had time to grapple with new material, and often, when you present the lesson again, students are ready to receive the information.

Once students understand a mini-lesson and can successfully complete the student practice activities, have them edit their own work. To call their attention to editing needs, place a check in the margin next to the line that requires repairs, or use the editing symbols below.

   Remember: Always have students edit for one item at a time. Structure this for them by listing on the chalkboard the order of items they should edit.

Editing   Symbols

Meaning	Example
Insert	I $\wedge$ happy. (am)
Upper Case (Capitalize)	leslie lopez
Lower Case	Çar
Transpose	recieve
Remove, Delete	She is not here
Indent For A Paragraph	#Once upon a time...
Add Period	Clean up ⊙
Add Comma	The sad $\wedge$ silent child wept.

Peer Content Editing Record

DATE: _____

WRITER'S NAME: _____

PEER EDITOR'S NAME: _____

TITLE OF PIECE: _____

FOCUS OF CONTENT EDITING: _____

_____

_____

_____

_____

_____

PEER EDITOR'S REACTION TO THE CONTENT:

_____

_____

_____

_____

_____

TEACHER'S COMMENTS:

_____

_____

_____

_____

_____

11 A Noun Plus an Apostrophe Shows Ownership

PURPOSE: To help students correctly use the apostrophe with nouns to show ownership.

Before Examples

1 On the pigs tails were red ribbons.

2 Snakes tugged at the hem of the princess gown.

3 Hanging from the seagulls beak was a man's finger.

4 The robbers suitcases contain stolen money.

5 The Roystons house is definitely haunted.

Revision Tips

1 Reread the sentence and look for the noun that shows ownership.

2 A noun showing possession is usually followed by another noun.

3 Circle the noun that needs an apostrophe.

4 Decide if the noun is singular or plural. Look at the verb to help you make this decision.

5 Add the apostrophe.

After Examples

1 On the pigs' tails were red ribbons.

2 Snakes tugged at the hem of the princess's gown.

3 Hanging from the seagull's beak was a man's finger.

4 The robbers' suitcases contain stolen money.

5 The Roystons' house is definitely haunted.

HELP BOX

Singular nouns form the possessive case by adding an 's: *child's bat; dog's leash; teacher's pen*

Plural nouns that end in s form the possessive case by adding an apostrophe: *friends' bikes; writers' books, princess's tiara.*

Plural nouns that don't end in s form the possessive case by adding 's: *deer's tracks, firemen's hoses, oxen's tail.*

Get Students Involved

ASK: "How does using the apostrophe to show possession clarify meaning? Do pronouns use apostrophes?" (No, personal pronouns change their spelling to show possession: *my, its, mine, you, yours, his, her, hers, our, ours, your, yours, their, theirs.*)

"Does the apostrophe form the plural of a noun?" (No, the apostrophe shows ownership, plural has to do with number—more than one.)

Student Practice 11

DIRECTIONS: In these sentences, locate nouns that should be in the possessive case. Rewrite adding apostrophes.

1. On the ledge of a high cliff were eagles nests.

2. While walking near the lake, the phantoms cape flapped in the wind.

3. The farmer repaired the oxens yokes.

4. The magicians suitcase contained many illusions.

REWRITE: _____

_____

_____

_____

_____

_____

_____

Student Practice 11A

1. Maxs stolen sneakers turned up in the basement of the school.

2. Scientists are breeding mices tail to extend three feet.

3. My younger sister hid in the ladies dress department.

4. Neither a bullet nor a ramming rod could puncture the Cyclops eye.

REWRITE: _____

_____

_____

_____

_____

_____

_____

12 Help Readers Know Who's Speaking

PURPOSE: To show students that when a speaker changes, it's time to start a new paragraph; to model how to use quotation marks and punctuation within dialogue; to show that no quotation marks are necessary when describing a character's inner thoughts

Before Example

The school bus stopped. Chantell climbed the two steps, looked down the aisle, and thought, I bet Maria did her math homework last night. Hi, Maria said Chantell. Can I sit next to you? Sure, answered Maria as she thought to herself that Chantell wants something today. So did you find the math homework as tough as I did asked Maria. Nope answered Chantell. Be a friend and let me see your work for the last three problems. I had to babysit my little brother and couldn't finish last night. Maria sat quietly. Please begged Chantell. I promise you can sit with our group at lunch whenever you want to. I'll help you do the last three. You don't have to copy mine said Maria. Well confessed Chantell, I didn't do any of it. Too late, said Maria, the bus is at school.

Revision Tips

1 Read the story and identify words such as *said*, *answered*, *replied*, *told*, *questioned*, *confessed*. These words tell you someone is speaking or thinking.

2 Find the speaker's words and place a check over the first and last word the speaker says.

3 Place quotation marks around the speaker's words.

4 Insert punctuation before the closing quotation marks (?, !).

5 Use words such as *thought*, *wondered*, and *told herself* to indicate inner dialogue. Use a comma between the thought and the thinker (,). Remember, you don't use quotation marks with inner thoughts.

6 Study the examples in the Help Box that illustrate how to punctuate direct quotations.

HELP BOX

Here are ways to write and punctuate direct quotations and inner thoughts. (Note, inner thoughts do not have quotation marks.)

- "Clean up your room right now," demanded Mother.

- Jimmie asked, "Can you come to the movies with me tomorrow?"

- "We lost the soccer game," the coach said, "but I'm proud of this team's exceptional sportsmanship."

- "The movie projector broke, so we walked home," said Tamika.

- I hope I can play in the tennis match, Vinnie thought.

90

After Example

The school bus stopped. Chantell climbed the two steps, looked down the aisle and thought, I bet Maria did her math homework last night. "Hi, Maria," said Chantell. "Can I sit next to you?"

"Sure," answered Maria as she thought to herself that Chantell wants something today.

"So, did you find the math homework as tough as I did?" asked Maria.

"Nope," answered Chantell. "Be a friend and let me see your work for the last three problems. I had to baby-sit my little brother and couldn't finish last night."

Maria sat quietly. "Please," begged Chantell. "I promise you can sit with our group at lunch whenever you want to."

"I'll help you do the last three. You don't have to copy mine," said Maria.

"Well," confessed Chantell, "I didn't do any of it."

"Too late," said Maria, "the bus is at school."

Get Students Involved

ASK: "How does separating the speakers help you read and understand the passage?" Discuss the different kinds of punctuation used with direct quotations in the Help Box and the After Example. "Can you locate inner thoughts? How do these give you a better handle on the character's mood or personality?"

Investigate How Authors Use Dialogue

Have students find a page of dialogue in their independent reading books and discuss the following questions:

◎ How does the author of your book punctuate dialogue?

◎ Does the dialogue give you information about the characters, the setting, or the plot?

◎ Are there examples of inner thoughts?

◎ What do you learn about the character from his or her thoughts?

Student Practice 12

DIRECTIONS: Rewrite the story so that the dialogue is written correctly.

Tamika wanted to go to the mall with Tillie more than anything. That rule my mom has about not going out on school nights is dumb thought Tamika. Maybe if I butter Mom up she'll let me go, Tamika told herself.

During dinner Tamika told her mom this is the best roasted chicken you've made. It's soft and so tasty. I'll have another piece. Glad you're enjoying it said Mom. And said Tamika, tonight I'll wash and dry the dishes and sweep the floor. You can watch the news. What is she up to wondered Mom. I always have to nag Tamika to help me. Bet she wants something, Mom thought.

After Tamika cleaned the kitchen, she walked into the TV room. Say Mom Tamika started, can I go to the mall with Tillie. Her mom's driving and coming. I did all my homework and we'll be gone only one hour. So that's it thought Tamika's Mom. You know the rule, Mom answered. Just this once begged Tamika. No answered Mom in a firm voice. Tamika stormed out of the room, stomped up the stairs, and slammed the door to her room.

REWRITE: _____

_____

_____

_____

_____

_____

_____

_____

_____

_____

_____

_____

_____

_____

13 Paragraphing a Narrative

PURPOSE: To help students understand that paragraphs help readers follow the plot of a narrative; to offer strategies that can help students understand when to start a new paragraph

Before Example ....

A TRIP TO GRANDMA'S

Janetta dragged her suitcase down the stairs, across the porch and helped her dad lift it into the trunk. "You've got enough in there for a month," Dad said, laughing out loud. "You're going to Grandma's for only two days." "I know," answered Janetta, "but Grandma is taking me out during the day and at night." Dad parked the car next to the train station. Crowded with people, the train station looked as if everyone in Cross Junction was traveling someplace. The ticket line looks like a snake slowly slithering across the yard, thought Janetta. Finally, Dad purchased a ticket for Janetta, and they walked to the waiting room. "I'll wait with you until it's time to board," said Dad. "I'll call tonight," said Janetta. Soon the conductor announced that Janetta's train was leaving in five minutes. She kissed and hugged her dad and followed the crowd down the steep stairs to the train track. Janetta lugged her suitcase into the train and quickly found a seat. I'm glad, she thought, Momma packed me a good lunch. Slowly, the train chugged out of the station. Faster and faster turned the wheels. Janetta watched Cross Junction disappear. In two hours, she'd be sitting with Grandma in the farmhouse kitchen. Janetta couldn't wait!

Revision Tips ....

1 Start a new paragraph when the speaker in a dialogue changes.

2 Start a new paragraph when the setting or place changes.

3 Start a new paragraph when the situation changes.

4 Start a new paragraph when time changes.

After Example ....

A TRIP TO GRANDMA'S

Janetta dragged her suitcase down the stairs, across the porch and helped her dad lift it into the trunk. "You've got enough in there for a month," Dad said, laughing out loud. "You're going to Grandma's for only two days."

"I know," answered Janetta, "but Grandma is taking me out during the day and at night."

Dad parked the car next to the train station. Crowded with people, the train station looked as if everyone in Cross Junction was traveling someplace. The ticket line looked like a snake slowly slithering across the yard, thought Janetta.

Finally, Dad purchased a ticket for Janetta, and they walked to the waiting room. "I'll wait with you until it's time to board," said Dad.

"I'll call tonight," said Janetta.

Soon the conductor announced that Janetta's train was leaving in five minutes. She kissed and hugged her dad and followed the crowd down the steep stairs to the train track. Janetta lugged her suitcase into the train and quickly found a seat.

I'm glad, she thought, Momma packed me a good lunch. Slowly, the train chugged out of the station. Faster and faster turned the wheels. Janetta watched Cross Junction disappear. In two hours, she'd be sitting with Grandma in the farmhouse kitchen. Janetta couldn't wait!

Get Students Involved . . . .

ASK: "How did paragraphing help you follow the plot? Understand the dialogue? How did the paragraph breaks follow the ideas listed in Revision Tips?"

Investigate How Authors Paragraph . . . .

Invite students to work with a partner or in small groups of three or four. Have them select two pages from a novel, short story, or folktale and discuss the way the author used paragraphing.

ASK: "Discuss the reasons you feel the author started a new paragraph. What have you learned about paragraphing a narrative story?"

Student Practice 13

DIRECTIONS: Separate the following paragraph into several paragraphs by placing the paragraph symbol (¶) next to the word that will start the next paragraph. Review the Revision Tips to refresh your memory.

Billy and Tony checked their hiking gear before they started up Whistler's Mountain. "Bug repellent, snake-bite kit, water, lunch, snacks," Tony said out loud as he removed and put into his backpack each item. Billy checked his and said, "I guess we're ready." This was the first time the boys had hiked without an adult. They felt good about hiking on the path up Whistler's Mountain because they'd done it more than five times with their dads. Cool and damp, the forest felt good after walking from home in the hot sun. Birds chirped and crickets hummed as they climbed, single file, along the trail. About noon when the sun, directly overhead, illumined the forest, Tony said, "Let's stop and eat. I'm starved." "Great idea," said Billy. The boys took out their lunch bags and water bottles, sat against a tree trunk, and ate. They shared Tony's chocolate chip cookies and Billy's fudge brownies. Suddenly, Billy stopped chewing. I'm scared, he thought, but I gotta tell Tony. In a quiet voice Billy said, "Hey, Tony, don't move. There's a snake above your head. Stay still. Be calm." Tony's sudden lurch forward was beyond his control. The snake, a copperhead, struck, biting Tony's upper arm. Screaming and sobbing, Tony grabbed his arm, feeling the pain extend toward his neck. The snake kit, get the snake kit, Billy repeated to himself. Quickly, he opened the kit, took out the tourniquet and knife, and went to work.

14 Paragraphing to Organize an Essay's Ideas

PURPOSE: To show that each paragraph in an essay contains details that support the main idea of the paragraph; to help students organize their ideas

Before Example

EATING-OUT JITTERS

"There are some foods that I'll never eat on a date." In my head I heard these words, spoken by my older sister, Sara, after I agreed to go to a fancy restaurant with my boyfriend, Rob. All week I worried about finding something to eat that wouldn't make noise or slide off my fork. All week I kept torturing myself by thinking about my first experience eating in public. My third-grade buddy, Sandra, lived in a fancy house in the country. Her mom invited me to spend the night, and I thought it would be great fun to swim in Sandra's pool and talk all night. Dinner changed my mind. You see, Sandra's mom was what I call "fancy." We ate in the dining room on a long table with flowers, china, and more spoons and forks at each place than I imagined existed. Soup was the first course, and I slurped my way through the entire bowl. Disaster struck when I received a plate of chicken and broccoli. I alternated picking up the broccoli and chicken breast with my hands and concentrated on chewing as quietly as possible. When I looked up, I saw Sandra and her mom and dad cutting their broccoli and chicken with a knife and fork. At that moment I decided never to eat with anyone but my family. Tonight, however, I would be sitting opposite Rob in a restaurant. Rob took me to the new Italian place. Just my luck, I thought, all they'll serve is spaghetti. How right I was! The list of spaghetti dishes was two pages: pasta with plain sauce, pasta with sausage, pasta with meatballs, pasta with seafood, etc. And I had to choose one. Actually, the evening turned out better than I expected. Rob taught me how to twirl the pasta with a fork and tablespoon, then pop it into my mouth. My nightmare of having pasta dripping from my mouth, on my jeans, and falling off my fork remained a dream. Eating out does not have to be a horrible experience as long as you know what you're doing. Now that I have conquered dining on spaghetti, I'm up to anything!

Revision Tips

1 Separate the introduction into its own paragraph.

2 Use the editing symbol to signal a new paragraph.

3 Introduce each paragraph, with a sentence that focuses readers on the topic the paragraph will discuss.

4 Make sure that the details in a paragraph relate to its main idea.

5 Present the details in a paragraph in a logical order.

6 Start a new paragraph when you switch to another idea.

7 Separate the conclusion into its own paragraph.

After Example . . . .

EATING-OUT JITTERS

"There are some foods that I'll never eat on a date." In my head I heard these words, spoken by my older sister, Sara, after I agreed to go to a fancy restaurant with my boyfriend, Rob. I worried about finding something to eat that wouldn't make noise or slide off my fork.

All week I kept torturing myself by thinking about my first experience eating in public. My third-grade buddy, Sandra, lived in a fancy house in the country. Her mom invited me to spend the night, and I thought it would be great fun to swim in Sandra's pool and talk all night. Dinner changed my mind. You see, Sandra's mom was what I call "fancy." We ate in the dining room on a long table with flowers, china, and more spoons and forks at each place than I imagined existed. Soup was the first course, and I slurped my way through the entire bowl. Disaster struck when I received a plate of chicken and broccoli. I alternated picking up the broccoli and chicken breast with my hands and concentrated on chewing as quietly as possible. When I looked up, I saw Sandra and her mom and dad cutting their broccoli and chicken with a knife and fork. At that moment I decided never to eat with anyone but my family.

Tonight, however, I would be sitting opposite Rob in a restaurant. Rob took me to the new Italian place. Just my luck, I thought. All they'll serve is spaghetti. How right I was! The list of spaghetti dishes was two pages: pasta with plain sauce, pasta with sausage, pasta with meatballs, pasta with seafood, etc. And I had to choose one.

Actually, the evening turned out better than I expected. Rob taught me how to twirl the pasta with a fork and tablespoon, then pop it into my mouth. My nightmare of having pasta dripping from my mouth, on my jeans, and falling off my fork remained a dream.

Eating out does not have to be a horrible experience as long as you know what you're doing. Now that I have conquered dining on spaghetti, I'm up to anything!

Get Students Involved . . . .

ASK: "Did separating paragraphs make reading the essay easier? Why?" Discuss the reasons used to decide on where to paragraph.

Student Practice 14

DIRECTIONS: The essay has been written as one long paragraph, yet it should be broken into several. Mark where each new paragraph starts, using the correct editing symbol (¶). Refresh your memory by rereading the Revision Tips.

Winter Is the Best

From my bedroom window, I watched the snow fall silently. Not a patch of ground could be seen. Heavy with snow, the trees' limbs curved toward the whitened ground. "No school," Mom shouted from the kitchen. A day to sleigh ride and build a snowman, I thought. That's why winter is my favorite season. Days off from school break the everyday routines of shower, breakfast, get dressed, and wait for the bus. While the snow falls, I put on two sweaters, a jacket, boots, a hat, and gloves. My friends Bobby and Richard meet me at the hill across from my house. First we trudge up and down the hill, packing the snow as tight as we can. Then we race down on our sleds. Sometimes we pile, one on top of the other, on one sled. Down the hill we whiz, falling off and rolling and laughing in the snow. After we've had enough of sledding, we're ready to build a snowman. Cold and moist, the snow is perfect for rolling into one large ball for the body and a smaller ball for the snowman's head. We all have a blast dressing the snowman. I put Dad's old fishing hat on its head. Bobby has two dark blue buttons for eyes, and Richard uses raisins to make a mouth. Into its mouth, Bobby pops an old corncob pipe. After I wrap a red scarf around its neck, we admire our work. Tired but happy, we trudge through the deep snow back to my house. There we drink hot chocolate to warm our bodies and think about how great it is to have a school snow day.

15 Using Colons Before Lists

PURPOSE: To help students understand a colon is used before listing items

Before Examples

1 James went shopping and purchased several items, a new computer mouse, a box of computer paper, some computer games, and disk labels.

2 For the Valentine's Day party, our class discussed having items such as; cookies, heart candies, soda, potato chips, napkins, paper cups and plates.

3 The dance is on Friday and we need the following, balloons, paper streamers, a boombox, taped recordings, and someone to DJ.

Revision Tips

1 Look for expressions that signal a list is coming.

2 Place a colon after the expression and before the list starts.

3 Check the greeting of a business letter to make sure you've used a colon.

After Examples

1 James went shopping and purchased the following: a new computer mouse, a box of computer paper, some computer games, and disk labels.

2 For the Valentine's Day party, our class discussed having items such as: cookies, heart candies, soda, potato chips, napkins, paper cups and plates.

3 The dance is on Friday and we need the following: balloons, paper streamers, a boombox, taped recordings, and someone to DJ.

Get Students Involved

ASK: "Did the colon signal a list that you should note? How can lists improve a piece of writing? Have you used colons? Why or why not?"

HELP BOX

◎ Use a colon before a list of items. These expressions might signal the need for a colon: *such as, like, as follows, the following.*

◎ Use a colon after a greeting or salutation in a business letter (use a comma in a friendly letter): *Dear Sir:, Dear Dr. Smith:, Gentlemen:.*

Student Practice 15

DIRECTIONS: For each situation, write sentences that contain lists; use a colon before the list.

- You're packing for a vacation.
- You're getting ready to bake cookies or a cake.
- You're thinking about gifts for someone's birthday.
- You're shopping for your school clothes.

WRITE: _____

_____

_____

_____

_____

_____

_____

_____

_____

_____

_____

_____

_____

_____

_____

_____

_____

_____

_____

_____

_____

Student Practice 15A

- ◉ You're a travel agent and you're telling a customer what to bring on a hiking trip in Canada.

- ◉ You're making a wish list for your birthday, Christmas, or Easter.

- ◉ You're listing all the animals you enjoyed visiting at the zoo.

- ◉ You need to clean you room. Make a list of all the things you have to do.

WRITE: _____

_____

_____

_____

_____

_____

_____

_____

_____

_____

_____

_____

_____

_____

_____

_____

16 Clarifying Series of Words and Phrases With Commas

PURPOSE: To show students how to use commas to separate a series of items, a series of phrases, and a series of adjectives

HELP BOX

- Use a comma to separate a list of items (1, 2, 6).
- Use a comma to separate two or more adjectives in front of a noun (3).
- Use a comma to separate a series of prepositional phrases (4, 5).

Before Examples

1 We packed a tablecloth paper plates sandwiches watermelon chocolate brownies and lemonade for our picnic in the park.

2 Next year I enter high school and will study algebra earth science world history English French and art.

3 The wizard of the forest is a clever secretive man.

4 Juan enjoyed riding on the merry-go-round on the Ferris wheel and on the roller coaster.

5 We found shells in the water on the sand and under rocks.

6 On our hike we saw deer copperheads a woodpecker and a bobcat.

Revision Tips

1 Reread, looking for a series of items with no commas and separate each item with a comma. Make sure you place a comma before the *and* or *or* that introduces the last item. <u>Example:</u> Mom baked cookies, <u>cupcakes, and</u> a chocolate cake.

2 Reread for a series of phrases that should be set off with commas.

3 Reread to check the number of adjectives used before a noun. If you've written two or more adjectives, then separate them with commas. Do not use a comma to separate the adjective immediately in front of the noun.

After Examples

1 We packed a tablecloth, paper plates, sandwiches, watermelon, chocolate brownies, and lemonade for our picnic in the park.

2 Next year I enter high school and will study algebra, earth science, world history, English, French, and art.

3 The wizard of the forest is a clever, secretive man.

4 Juan enjoyed riding on the merry-go-round, on the Ferris wheel, and on the roller coaster.

5 We found shells in the water, on the sand, and under rocks.

6 On our hike we saw deer, copperheads, a woodpecker, and a bobcat.

Get Students Involved

ASK: "How did commas help clarify meaning and make reading the sentences easier?"

Student Practice 16

DIRECTIONS: Write original sentences for each of the four prompts. Place commas correctly.

1 Write about your favorite bands, singers, or books. Include a series of items.

2 Describe an alien using two or more adjectives.

3 Use three or more phrases to explain where you walked.

4 Explain what you packed for your camping trip.

WRITE: _____

_____

_____

_____

_____

_____

_____

_____

_____

_____

_____

_____

_____

_____

_____

_____

_____

Student Practice 16A

1 Write a sentence naming three to five places you'd like to visit.

2 Use two or more adjectives to describe your favorite or least favorite food.

3 Use three or more phrases to tell where you looked for your lost ring.

3 Write a sentence that lists four to five instruments you saw at a parade.

WRITE: _____

_____

_____

_____

_____

_____

_____

_____

_____

_____

_____

_____

_____

_____

_____

_____

_____

_____

Grammar Lessons and Strategies Scholastic Professional Books

17 Using Commas to Set Off Expressions and Direct Addresses

PURPOSE: To show students how to use commas in direct address and when sentences open with expressions like *well, yes, no, why, finally, however*

Before Examples

1 John it's your turn to clean the horses' stalls.

2 Why I'm surprised that you haven't learned to ride a two-wheel bike.

3 Finally the spacecraft lifted off the launching pad and zoomed toward Saturn.

4 Clean up your room now Jill.

5 Yes both of you may go to the movies this afternoon.

6 No you cannot go to the lake alone because you can't swim.

HELP BOX

When starting a sentence with one of the following expressions, set each off with a comma: **in fact, however, finally, in my opinion, nevertheless, to tell the truth, for example, of course.**

Revision Tips

1 If a sentence opens with *well, yes, no, why,* place a comma after the word.

2 Don't follow words such as *well, yes, no, why* with a comma if they do not interrupt the sentence. Example: Why aren't you coming to the party?

3 If you directly address a person in the opening of a sentence, place a comma after that person's name.

4 If you directly address a person at the end of a sentence, place the comma before that person's name.

After Examples

1 John, it's your turn to clean the horses' stalls.

2 Why, I'm surprised that you haven't learned to ride a two-wheel bike.

3 Finally, the spacecraft lifted off the launching pad and zoomed toward Saturn.

4 Clean up your room now, Jill.

5 Yes, both of you may go to the movies this afternoon.

6 No, you cannot go to the lake alone because you can't swim.

Get Students Involved

ASK: "How do the commas improve your understanding of these sentences?"

Student Practice 17

DIRECTIONS: Correctly place commas when writing the following sentences:

1 Start a sentence with *finally.*_____

2 Start a sentence with *yes* or *no.*_____

3 Open a sentence with *well* or *why.*_____

4 Open a sentence with *in my opinion.*_____

Student Practice 17A

DIRECTIONS: Read the paragraph below and edit for commas, placing a comma where needed. The paragraph will have items in a series, more than two adjectives, and sentences that start with the expressions you learned in Mini-Lesson 17. Edit for one item at a time.

Dad and I packed for our day's canoe trip down the Shenandoah River. We took two life jackets several sandwiches fruit cookies and four bottles of drinking water. After loading the canoe on a small sandy beach, we pushed it into the river and jumped in. Finally I thought the canoe trip I've waited for because this was the season when rapids dotted the river. Well it didn't take long for us to meet churning water and sharp jutting rocks. Dad shouted orders and I followed them quickly, because I didn't want our supplies and ourselves dumped in the water.

MINI-LESSON
18 Repairing Run-on Sentences

PURPOSE: To teach students to identify and repair sentences that attempt to carry too many ideas or contain two or more sentences joined incorrectly

Before Examples

1 While fishing Jim felt hungry he picked a worm from the can and ate his midday snack.

2 A gray mist covered the graveyard when we entered and our flashlights were useless as the fog thickened so we decided to walk along the path and flash the light onto every grave until we found the one marked with a skull and bones.

Revision Tips

Use these methods to fix sentence 1 and similar sentences:

1 Create complete sentences by adding periods and capital letters.

2 Add one of the connecting words from the Help Box to create a compound sentence. A compound sentence consists of two independent, related sentences joined by a conjunction (see page 76). If you keep the subject in the new second sentence, you will need a comma after the connecting word.

3 Separate the two parts of a run-on with a semicolon (;), which takes the place of a period or a connecting word.

Use these methods to fix sentence 2 and similar sentences:

4 Rearrange sentences that are too long and contain ideas that don't relate to the main purpose of the sentence.

5 Create two sentences out of one that switches ideas or changes time or place.

HELP BOX

and
but
so
although
yet
as
when
since
before
while

After Examples

Here are four ways to rewrite sentence 1:

1 Create two complete sentences.
While fishing, Jim felt hungry. He picked a worm from the can and ate his midday snack.

2 Add a connecting word and remove the subject of the second sentence.
While fishing, Jim felt hungry, picked a worm from the can and ate his midday snack.

3 Add a connecting word and a comma and keep the subject of the second sentence.

While fishing, Jim felt hungry, so he picked a worm from the can and ate his midday snack.

4 Use a semicolon (;) instead of a connecting word.

While fishing, Jim felt hungry; he picked a worm from the can and ate his midday snack.

Here is one way to rewrite sentence 2:

A gray mist covered the graveyard when we entered. As the fog thickened, our flashlights became useless, so we stuck to the path. Our flashlights illuminated every grave until we found the one marked with a skull and bones.

Editing Tips for Run-on Sentences . . . .

1 When a sentence in your writing covers three or more lines on your paper, test it for a run-on.

2 A sentence that contains several unrelated ideas is a run-on.

3 A sentence that contains too many ideas and rambles on is a run-on.

4 Two independent sentences without a semicolon, conjunction, or period create a run-on.

5 A sentence that switches from one place or one time to another can be a run-on.

Get Students Involved . . . .

ASK: "Can you explain what can cause a run-on sentence? How can you locate run-ons in your own writing? Why do run-ons confuse readers? Can you rewrite the second sentence and improve on the After Example? Why was yours better?"

Student Practice 18

DIRECTIONS: Rewrite the sentence four different ways.

Our class party and picnic was at Spring Lake we swam, jumped off the diving board, and ate dozens of hamburgers.

REWRITE: _____

_____

_____

_____

_____

_____

_____

_____

Student Practice 18A

DIRECTIONS: Repair the run-on sentence using any strategies you've learned.

Tanisha looked down the steep ski slope she frowned and appeared reluctant to start because this was her second time skiing.

REWRITE: _____

_____

_____

Student Practice 18B

DIRECTIONS: Rewrite and repair the shifts in time and place and events.

Jennell flew to Chicago to see her grandmother this morning and then in the evening she took a train to Canada and camped out in the mountains for three weeks.

REWRITE: _____

_____

_____

19 Turn Sentence Fragments Into Complete Sentences

PURPOSE: To show students that a sentence is considered a fragment when it doesn't express a complete thought; to show students how to turn fragments into complete sentences

Before Examples . . . .

1 Although Peter won the individual track title.

2 Frightened by lightning.

3 By the lake in the park.

Revision Tips . . . .

For fragment 1:
When a subordinate clause stands alone, it is a fragment. Complete the clause by explaining why or how Peter won the title.

For fragment 2:
When a participial phrase stands alone, it is a fragment. Complete the participial phrase by telling who was frightened and what he or she did.

For fragment 3:
Two prepositional phrases are a fragment because they don't express a complete thought. Tell what occurred, and the prepositional phrases become part of a complete thought.

After Examples . . . .

1 Although Peter won the individual track title, he was saddened that his team came in second.

2 The dog, frightened by the lightning, hid under the bed.

3 A ghost stepped out of the mist that covered the walking path by the lake in the park.

Get Students Involved . . . .

ASK: "Can you explain what can cause a fragment? Why do fragments confuse readers? Why are the After Examples clearer? Can you revise the fragments? Why was yours better?"

Student Practice 19

DIRECTIONS: Rewrite these fragments so they contain a complete thought.

1 Since his birthday party.

2 Bitten by a rabid dog.

3 Around the corner from your house.

4 Until the package arrives.

REWRITE: _____

_____

_____

_____

_____

_____

_____

Student Practice 19A

DIRECTIONS: Underline the fragments in this paragraph and rewrite each one.

  A fight between two students occurred in the locker room. Since Anthony took José's shorts. Angry because he was unprepared for gym class, José got even in the locker room. In front of his locker after showering. Anthony swore he would never take something from Anthony again.

REWRITE: _____

_____

_____

_____

_____

_____

_____

20 Eliminate the Passive Voice

PURPOSE: To show students that when *am, is, was, were* precede action verbs, the combination forms the passive voice; to change the passive voice into the active voice, creating sentences that grab the reader

Before Examples

1 I <u>was interviewed</u> by the head of the fishery for a summer job on a fishing boat.

2 That entire village <u>was destroyed</u> by flooding from a hurricane.

3 Three children <u>were bitten</u> by a rabid dog and <u>were taken</u> to the hospital by ambulance.

4 A banana <u>is eaten</u> by that monkey every day.

Revision Tips

1 Underline the verb in the passive voice.

2 Eliminate the helping verbs: am, is, are, was, were.

3 Rearrange the words in the sentence by eliminating the helping verbs and making the verb active. You might have to change some words.

After Examples

1 The head of the fishery interviewed me for a summer job on a fishing boat.

2 Flooding from a hurricane destroyed that entire village.

3 A rabid dog bit three children who rode to the hospital in an ambulance.

4 That monkey eats a banana every day.

Get Students Involved

ASK: "How does the active voice improve the sentence?" It creates a sense of immediacy and energy; it clearly conveys the action. "Are the sentence openings more varied? Why did you have to rearrange some words?"

> **IDEA BOX**
>
> | | |
> |---|---|
> | | were bitten—bit |
> | was interviewed—interviewed | were taken—rode |
> | was destroyed—destroyed | is eaten—eats |

Student Practice 20

DIRECTIONS: Rewrite, changing the underlined verbs to the active voice. It's okay to rearrange, add, or delete words when you rewrite.

1 The rider <u>was thrown</u> off the horse while jumping across a stream.

_____

_____

2 Angelina <u>was stung</u> by a huge bee today.

_____

3 I <u>am frightened</u> of driving through a lightning storm.

_____

4 Those kittens <u>were abandoned</u> by the family that lives in the apartment below mine.

_____

_____

Student Practice 20A

Carlos and Ramon <u>were taken</u> to a secret hiding place by David. The two boys <u>were blindfolded</u> and <u>were marched</u> toward the hiding place. The hiding place, an old, wooden shack, <u>was packed</u> with cardboard cartons. Carlos and Ramon <u>were told</u> by David that they could not remove their blindfolds until the sun set.

REWRITE: _____

_____

_____

_____

_____

_____

_____

_____

_____

Honing Students' Editing Skills

It was mid-January, my first visit to a fifth-grade class in a nearby school. The teacher, a young woman, was completing her first year. As I circulated, pausing at each desk while students wrote, I noticed several students recopying pieces that had been corrected in red ink. Who's improving here? I wondered. My own junior high school days flashed before me. At first, anger would fill me when my teacher handed back paper after paper marked in red ink. Then, I became indifferent, thinking, If Mr. D. wants to do all the work, let him. All I have to do is recopy—no thinking and sweat here.

Editing is tough for students. It's difficult for them to find errors. In fact, it's rare for students in grades four to nine to be able to edit a piece to perfection. Teachers who reduce students' grades by removing ten points for every missing comma or fragment or run-on create anxiety and frustration, make editing a task to be avoided, and inhibit students from experimenting with more complex sentence structures.

I correct only a part of a student's paper if I'm working one on one and want to model my thinking processes. The student completes the rest of the editing, sometimes independently, other times with my prompting. I also recognize that students cannot catch every error. Even professional writers have editors and copy editors who refine a manuscript for punctuation and usage. Here are some editing suggestions that I reflect on several times a year:

- Don't correct students' papers, or you're the one who improves.

- Let students edit and correct—that's how they become proficient proofreaders.

- Have students read their work out loud and follow the text with a pencil. This enables them to spot omitted words, misused words, repeated words and phrases, passive voice, and missing punctuation.

- Invite students to edit for two to three items, looking for one item at a time.

- Let perfection go and step in only to support students with pieces that will be published. When students publish a piece, you take on the role of editor in a publishing house.

- Present mini-lessons and demonstrate how you go about editing.

- Scaffold editing for students who can't pinpoint their errors or for those who have made so many errors that working alone is difficult and daunting.

- Allow enough time for students to edit in class where you, the expert, can offer support.

Becoming a capable proofreader and editor takes time and practice. The best way for students to improve is to edit their own writing, support a peer who is editing, and know that the teacher is available for one-on-one guidance.

References

Baumann, James F., Leah A. Jones, and Nancy Seifert-Kessel. 1993. "Using Think Alouds to Enhance Children's Comprehension Monitoring Abilities." *The Reading Teacher*, 47: 187–199.

Brinkley, Ellen. "Learning to Use Grammar with Precision Through Editing Conferences."*Lessons to Share: On Teaching Grammar in Context*, edited by Constance Weaver. Portsmouth, NH: Boynton/Cook.

Calkins, Lucy M. 1980. "When Children Want to Punctuate: Basic Skills Belong in Context." *Language Arts*, 57: 567-573.

_____. 1983. *Lessons From a Child*. Portsmouth, NH: Heinemann.

_____. 1994, *The Art of Teaching Writing*. Portsmouth, NH: Heinemann.

DeBoer, J. J. 1959. "Grammar in Language Teaching." *Elementary English* 36: 413-421.

Graves, Donald H. 1994. *A Fresh Look at Writing*. Portsmouth, NH: Heinemann.

Greene, H. A. 1950. "English—Language, Grammar, and Composition." *Encyclopedia of Educational Research*. (rev. ed., edited by W. S. Monroe) New York: Macmillan.

Lytle, Susan L. 1982. "Exploring Comprehension Style: A Study of Twelfth Grade Readers' Transactions with Text." Ph.D. diss., University of Pennsylvania.

Noden, Harry R. 1999. *Image Grammar: Using Grammatical Structures to Teach Writing*. Portsmouth, NH: Boynton/Cook, Heinemann.

Robb, Laura. 1998. *Easy-to-Manage Reading & Writing Conferences*. New York: Scholastic.

_____. 1999. *Brighten Up Boring Beginnings and Other Quick Writing Lessons*. New York: Scholastic.

Rosenblatt, Louise. *Literature as Exploration,* 4th ed. 1983. New York: Modern Language Association of America.

_____. 1978. *The Reader, the Text, and the Poem: The Transactional Theory of the Literary Work*. Carbondale, Il. SIU Press.

Searles, J. R. and G. R. Carlson. 1960. "Language, Grammar, and Composition." *Encyclopedia of Educational Research*, (3rd ed, edited by C.W. Harris) New York: Macmillan.

Warriner, John E. 1986. *English Grammar and Composition* (2nd course). San Diego, CA: Harcourt.

Weaver, Constance. 1996. *Teaching Grammar in Context*. Portsmouth, NH: Boynton/Cook, Heinemann.

Weaver, Constance. 1998. "Teaching Grammar in the Context of Writing." *Lessons to Share: On Teaching Grammar in Context*, edited by Constance Weaver. Portsmouth, NH: Boynton/Cook, Heinemann.

Literature Cited

Babbitt, Natalie. 1977. *The Eyes of the Amaryllis*. New York: Farrar, Straus & Giroux.

_____. 1973. *Tuck Everlasting*. New York: Farrar, Straus, & Giroux.

Begay, Shonto. 1995. NAVAJO: *Visions and Voices Across the Mesa*. New York: Scholastic.

Cadnum, Michael. 2000. *HEAT*. New York: Viking.

Carlstrom, Nancy White. 1998. *Midnight Dance of the Snowshoe Hare*: *Poems of Alaska*. Illustrated by Ken Kuroi. New York: Philomel.

Caseley, Judith. 2000. *Playing to A.L.* New York: Greenwillow.

Dickinson, Emily. 1934. *Poems for Youth*. Edited by Alfred Leete Hampson. Boston: Little, Brown.

Feelings, Tom, ed. 1993. *Soul Looks Back in Wonder*. New York: Dial.

Freedman, Rusell. 1987. *Lincoln: A Photobiography.* New York: Clarion.

Garland, Sherry. 2000. *Voices of the Alamo*. Illustrated by Ronald Himler. New York: Scholastic.

Grimes, Nikki. 2000. *A Dime a Dozen*, Pictures by Angelo. New York: Dial.

Hamilton, Virginia. 1985. *The People Could Fly: American Black Folktales*. Illustratoed by Leo and Diane Dillon. New York: Knopf.

Hobbs, Will. 1997. *Ghost Canoe*. New York: William Morrow.

Jean-Pierre, Sherley. 1999. "Quilted Soul.*" Quiet Storm: Voices of Young Black Poets*. Edited by Lydia Omolola Okutoro. New York: Hyperion.

Kent, Peter. 1998. *Hidden Under the Ground: The World Beneath Your Feet*. New York: Dutton.

Lasky, Kathryn. 1995. *She's Wearing a Dead Bird on Her Head!*. New York: Hyperion.

_____. 1996. *True North: A Novel of the Underground Railroad*. New York: Scholastic.

Lester, Julius. 1972. *Long Journey Home: Stories from Black History*. New York: Dial.

Lowry, Lois. 1993. *The Giver*. Boston: Houghton Mifflin.

Marcellino, Fred. 1999. *I Crocodile*. New York: HarperCollins.

Myers, Walter Dean. 1996. *SLAM!* New York: Scholastic.

_____. 1997. *Harlem*. Illustrated by Christopher Myers. New York: Scholastic.

Naidoo, Beverly. 1995. *No Turning Back: A Novel of South Africa*. New York: HarperCollins.

Paterson, Katherine. 1974. *Of Nightingales That Weep*. New York: Crowell.

_____. 1980. *Jacob Have I Loved*. New York: Crowell.

_____. 1973. *The Sign of the Chrysanthemum*. New York: Crowell.

_____. 1980. *Jacob Have I Loved*. New York: Crowell.

_____. 1978. *The Great Gilly Hopkins*. New York: Crowell

Pinkney, Andrea Davis. 1998. *Duke Ellington*. New York: Hyperion.

Soto, Gary. 1990. *Baseball in April and Other Stories*. New York: Harcourt, Brace & Company.

Van Leeuwen, Jean. 1994. *Bound for Oregon*. New York: Dial.

Walker, Margaret. 1993. "Mother of Brown-Ness," in *Soul Looks Back in Wonder*, Tom Feelings, editor and illustrator.

Walter, Mildred Pitts. 1996. *Second Daughter: The Story of a Slave Girl*. New York: Scholastic.

Wisniewski, David. 1996. *Golem*. Boston: Houghton Mifflin.

Yolen, Jane. 1987. *Owl Moon*. Illustrated by John Shoenherr. New York: Philomel.

Guidelines and Forms for Peer Editing and Writing

PURPOSE: To offer students editing experiences that guide their reading; to provide partners with useful feedback as well as to fine tune students' proofreading and content editing skills.

Introduction

"When I ask my students to peer edit," a seventh grade teacher told me, "all they do is write phrases like 'Good job! Nice work. I liked it!' They never offer the kind of feedback that helps the writer improve." My initial forays into peer editing reaped similar results. Inviting students to peer edit is not enough. Student writers need specific guidelines that show them what to look for and how to read and respond to a peer's piece.

Guidelines you set for students prior to drafting a piece always provide items for peer editing. However, do not ask students to peer edit for all the content and writing convention guidelines you've established with them. The task is too daunting. Start fourth and fifth graders with one to two content items and one to two writing convention items to peer edit. Students in grades six through eight can handle more at the start. How much to ask students to do is your judgment call; it depends on their experiences and background knowledge.

The peer editing forms on pages 120–121 are designed for younger grades and the forms on pages 122–124 are for older students. Adapt them to your needs. Then develop peer editing forms that relate to the writing guidelines you and students have negotiated.

Peer Editing Sheet

Date: _____

Name of Peer Editor: _____

Name of Author: _____

Title of the Piece You are Editing: _____

Read the story:

◎ Put a check in the margin next to two places that need more details.

◎ List some details you think might help the author.

Possible Details for First Check:

_____

_____

_____

_____

_____

Possible Details for Second Check:

_____

_____

_____

_____

_____

Use editing symbols to show the following:

◎ Need for capital letter at start of sentences.

◎ Mark places where a new paragraph should start.

Grammar Lessons and Strategies Scholastic Professional Books

Peer Editing Sheet

Date: _____

Name of Peer Editor: _____

Name of Author: _____

Title of the Piece You are Editing: _____

Read the entire piece.

Read the topic sentence. Did it state the topic in an interesting way?

_____

Should the author write two to three other topic sentences?

_____

List the information you feel the author should include in the topic sentence:

_____

_____

_____

_____

Did the information in the body relate to and support each topic sentence?

_____

_____

Can you suggest some ideas the author can think about that might improve this part?

_____

_____

Circle words you feel are misspelled.

Use editing symbols to show the need for commas in a series.

Peer Editing Sheet

Date: _____

Name of Peer Editor: _____

Name of Author: _____

Title of the Piece You are Editing: _____

Content and Form Checklist:

Look for the following and check if all is in good order.

_____ There are three separate paragraphs.

_____ The introduction contains the title and author.

_____ The introduction contains a general opening sentence and thesis.

_____ The introduction ends with a transition sentence to the second paragraph.

_____ Paragraph two opens with a general, introductory sentence.

_____ There are three specific pieces of support in paragraph two.

_____ Ideas are presented in a logical order.

_____ Paragraph two makes connections between the support and the thesis.

_____ There is a concluding paragraph.

Writing Conventions Checklist—use editing symbols to mark the following:

_____ Complete sentences.

_____ Used quotes correctly.

_____ Used capital letters correctly.

_____ Commas placed where they belong.

Offer one to two suggestions that could improve this piece:

_____

_____

_____

Grammar Lessons and Strategies Scholastic Professional Books

Peer Editing Sheet

Date: _____

Name of Peer Editor: _____

Name of Author: _____

Title of the Piece You are Editing: _____

Read the story once and comment on these items:

Does the title fit the story? Should the author think of other possible titles?

_____

_____

_____

What is the problem the main character faces?

_____

_____

_____

Name the main character and describe his/her personality by completing the chart:

Main Character	Personality Trait	Part of the Story that Showed this Trait

Did the ending fit the story? If not, list some ideas the author could consider:

_____

_____

_____

_____

Writing convention checklist—use editing symbols to mark the following:

_____ Wrote direct quotations correctly.

_____ Used apostrophe with contractions and to show possession.

Peer Editing Sheet

Date: _____

Name of Peer Editor: _____

Name of Author: _____

Title of the Piece You are Editing: _____

Read the story:

Did the title work for you?

_____

Should the author try writing one to two alternate titles?

_____

Put a check in the margin next to two places that TELL instead of SHOW.

List some details you think might help the author.

_____

_____

_____

Possible Showing Details for First Check:

_____

_____

_____

Possible Showing Details for Second Check:

_____

_____

_____

Writing Convention Checklist—use editing symbols to mark the following:

_____ The piece has paragraphing

_____ Commas are placed correctly for compound sentences and introductory phrase or clauses.

Grammar Lessons and Strategies Scholastic Professional Books

Literary Example Lessons for the Overhead

PURPOSE: To provide teachers with excerpts from the finest children's literature that they can use as models when teaching specific nouns, adjectives, and strong verbs

Introduction

Again and again, I find myself sharing selections from fiction, nonfiction, and poetry. I think of these selections as mentors that can help students gain deeper insights into the writers' craft. The more students observe and talk about these literary examples, the easier it becomes for them to understand what they've learned from reading and thinking and begin to connect it to their own writing.

The three pages that follow can be transformed into overhead transparencies. If you don't have access to an overhead projector, print some of the examples on chart paper and share with students.

Involve students in collecting short selections from their reading that illustrate an author's use of specific nouns,adjectives, and strong verbs, as well as varying the opening of sentences with prepositional phrases or clauses. Set aside time for students to share their findings in groups of three to five. Then ask each group to select a top-notch example and record it on a piece of large chart paper or construction paper.

SPECIFIC NOUNS

The rosebushes of shame on his face became bouquets of love.
(Page 74)

— "Seventh Grade" from *Baseball in April* by Gary Soto.

That morning dozens of politicians and their wives,
newspapermen, and other spectators drove down from
Washington in buggies and carriages to watch their army defeat
the rebels. They brought along picnic baskets, champagne, and
opera glasses, camped on a hillside, and waited for the action
to begin.

—*Abraham Lincoln: A Photobiography* by Russell Freedman

Using my precious crab money, I went to Kellam's and bought a
bottle of Jergens Lotion, emery boards, orange sticks, cuticle
remover, even a bottle of fingernail polish, which though
colorless, seemed a daring purchase. (page 129)

— from *Jacob Have I Loved* by Katherine Paterson

Throngs of people crowd the parking lot
Aroma of mutton stew and fried bread
Mingles with the fragrance
    of cotton candy and popcorn
Today the tribal fair begins

— "Many Faces, Many Stories" from *NAVAJO: Visions and
Voices Across the Mesa* by Shonto Begay

SPECIFIC ADJECTIVES

The fellow look at the foot of his bed. He's seein two little pointy ears comin up over the edige of the bed. In another minute, he's seein two big, scary-red eyeballs lookin straight at him. (page 119)

— "The Peculiar Such Thing" from *The People Could Fly*, by Virginia Hamilton

But then I saw the crumpled Kleenex in Cindy's hand, a white tissue so wadded and worn it was nearly reduced to lint. (page 75)

— from *Heat* by Michael Cadnum

With six small diamonds for his eyes
He walks upon the summer skies,
Drawing from his silken blouse
The lacework of his dwelling house.

— from *The Spider* by Robert P. Tristram Coffin

It [the road] wandered along in curves and easy angles, swayed off and up in a pleasant tangent to the top of a small hill, ambled down again between fringes of bee-hung clover, and then cut sidewise across a meadow. (page 5)

— from *Tuck Everlasting* by Natalie Babbitt

The bathroom had been painted a lemony yellow, which made the old pink towels look like limp, grimy flags against the gleaming sunshine. (page 55)

— from *Praying To A.L.* by Judith Caseley

STRONG VERBS

He hunched his shoulders and tried to make himself smaller in the seat. He wanted to disappear, to fade away, not to exist. He didn't dare to turn and find his parents in the crowd. He couldn't bear to see their faces darkened with shame. (page 58)

—from *The Giver* by Lois Lowry

I could hear a low indistinct murmur of talk from the nest wagon. A horse gave a muffled whinny. A touch of breeze rustled the wagon cover for a moment, then moved away. Somewhere far off a wolf howled. (pages 112-113)

—from *Bound for Oregon* by Jean Van Leeuwen

The two ladies swallowed their disgust and muffled their anger.

—from *She's Wearing a Dead Bird on Her Head!* by Kathryn Lasky

Weather is full
of the nicest sounds:
it sings
 and rustles
and pings
and pounds
and hums
and tinkles
and strums
and twangs...

—from "Weather is Full of the Nicest Sounds" by Aileen Fisher